PRECIOUS TIME

THE PSYCHOLOGY OF EFFECTIVE PARENTING
WITH PARENTING PLANS

DR. GALEN E. COLE
with Skot Waldron

Although the author and publisher have made every effort to ensure the accuracy and completeness of the information contained in this book, we assume no responsibility for errors, inaccuracies, omissions, or inconsistencies herein. Any slights of people, places, or organizations are unintentional.

Cole, Dr. Galen E.
Precious Time

ISBN No. 1453757805

TABLE OF CONTENTS

SECTION I. **HOW TO DEVELOP AND IMPLEMENT AN EFFECTIVE PARENTING PLAN** **15**

Chapter 1   The Parenting Logic Model   16
Chapter 2   Developing a Family Management Plan   23
Chapter 3   Developing a "Family Brand" *by Skot Waldron*   24
Chapter 4   How to Develop a Family Goal Statement   33
Chapter 5   The Planning and Organizing Guide   36
Chapter 6   Setting and Justifying Family Rules   43
Chapter 7   How to Enforce Family Rules   49
Chapter 8   Motivating and Rewarding Desirable Behaviors   59
Chapter 9   Contracting for Performance   66
Chapter 10   Evaluating Performance   69
Chapter 11   Building and Maintaining Healthy Relationships   71
Chapter 12   Principles of Good Interpersonal Communication   77
Chapter 13   Message Mapping: A Strategy for Communicating Around High Concern Issues   84
Chapter 14   Counseling Your Children   92
Chapter 15   Mediating Conflicts   96

SECTION II. **TEACHING TO ENSURE GOOD HEALTH AND GOOD CHARACTER** **97**

Chapter 16   Deciding What to Teach   99
Chapter 17   Teaching Methods   107
Chapter 18   Developmental Considerations in Teaching   113
Chapter 19   Psychological Considerations in Teaching   115
Chapter 20   Creating an Environment for Learning   118
Chapter 21   Preparing a Lesson Plan   119
Chapter 22   Sample Lesson Plans   122
Chapter 23   Conclusion and Summary   209

TABLES AND TOOLS

Table 3.1	Family Branding Guide	27
Table 4.1	Sample Family Goal Statement	34
Table 5.1	Planning and Organizing Guide	37
Table 5.2	Sample Family Plan #1 Using the POG	38
Table 5.3	Sample Family Plan #2 Using the POG	40
Table 6.1	Family Rule Development Guide	45
Table 6.2	Sample Family Rule Development Guide	46
Table 8.1	Chore and Activity Chart	64
Table 8.2	Index Card Reinforcer Chart	65
Table 9.1	Parent/Child Contract	66
Table 9.2	Sample Parent/Child Contract	67
Table 11.1	The Family Sentiment Building Guide	72
Table 11.2	Sample Family Sentiment Building Guide	73
Table 12.1	Activity Request Form	80
Table 13.1	Message Map on a Question About Sex	87
Table 13.2	Message Map on a Underage Drinking and Driving	89
Table 15.1	Conflict Mediation Strategy	96
Table 16.1	Lesson Ideas	101
Table 16.2	Progress Tracker	104
Table 19.1	Psychological Conditions Important to Behavioral Compliance	116
Table 21.1	How to Develop a Lesson Plan	121
Table 22.1	The Problem Solving Planner	203

SAMPLE LESSON PLANS

Lesson 1	We Want to Have an Ideal Family	123
Lesson 2	We Believe in Being Honest	125
Lesson 3	We Believe in Making and Saving Money	127
Lesson 4	We Believe in Watching Our Words	130
Lesson 5	We Believe in Being Grateful	134
Lesson 6	Developing and Maintaining Spirituality	136
Lesson 7	We Believe in Being Media Literate	139
Lesson 8	How to Correlate and Calendar Family Activities	143
Lesson 9	We Believe in Setting Goals	145
Lesson 10	We Believe in Showing Kindness to Everyone	148
Lesson 11	Accepting Discipline With a Good Attitude	151
Lesson 12	Developing Proper Grooming Habits	155
Lesson 13	Recognizing and Managing Stress	157
Lesson 14	Understand That We Are What We Eat	160
Lesson 15	How to Get and Keep Positive Self-Esteem	162
Lesson 16	Developing Strategies to Resist Peer Pressure	166
Lesson 17	Preventing Drug Use	170
Lesson 18	Delaying Sex Until Marriage	172
Lesson 19	Learning and Practicing Self-Control	174
Lesson 20	Practicing Self-Directed Change	178
Lesson 21	Learning to Control Thoughts and Practice Cognitive Restructuring	183
Lesson 22	Acquiring the Dimensions of Health and Well-Being	186
Lesson 23	Thinking and Feeling: The Key to Positive Emotions	194
Lesson 24	Developing Problem Solving	200
Lesson 25	Increasing Spirituality and Using Prayer	207

ACKNOWLEDGEMENTS

I acknowledge my parents and grandparents for the collective wisdom they have passed on to me about how to raise healthy, responsible children. I especially acknowledge my wife, Priscilla, for her untiring efforts to teach and develop healthy relationships with each of our five children. Finally, I thank each of my children, Amanda, Zachary, Nicholes, Joshua, and Jordan for their respect and willingness to be taught by a father who has his share of imperfections, but who loves each of them unconditionally.

Galen Cole

The examples in my life for strong family bonds and great love are numerous. I'd like to thank Christi for loving me more than anyone else could, and trying hard every day to be the perfect wife and mother. Thanks to my parents for always being a huge part of my life, even when we were hundreds of miles apart. Thank you Galen for giving me the opportunity to add my insight, and giving me insight at the same time, about what branding means for all of us. Last, I'd like to thank my little girl Tallulah for giving me the incredible opportunity to be a father.

Skot Waldron

We'd also like to thank Shannon Howard for her hard work and diligence in editing this book. Her direction and professionalism are greatly appreciated.

INTRODUCTION

T here is a lot they do not tell you when you become a parent. One thing *they* (in my case, *they* was actually a nurse in the delivery room when my first child was born) did tell me is that there is no instruction book for raising children. When I heard this the first time, it did not make sense. Surely someone wrote an instruction manual for the important task of parenthood. After some research I discovered that many such instruction manuals have been written and most of them have included the word *Parenting* in the title of the book.

After reading many of these parenting books and parenting five children, I decided that something was missing in each instruction manual. I was not exactly sure what *it* was until I discovered the missing component during a therapy session with a family who was struggling with many difficult problems. I suggested that the family should list their family goals and develop a plan that they could follow to achieve these milestones. The parents followed my recommendation and developed what I now call a *Parenting Plan*. In the next session they presented their plan to me so they could get feedback on their ideas. From the outset of this follow-up session, it was obvious that the process of simply developing their plan had given these parents a sense of hope. In previous sessions they were very discouraged and tended to focus on specific problems they were experiencing with their children; however, in this session they were upbeat and encouraged by the fact that they now had a plan for moving forward. In subsequent sessions the couple continued to make progress as they implemented and refined their plan.

This process of helping a couple design, implement, and refine a *Parenting Plan* has been duplicated many times in my practice as well as in my home. My wife and I have developed family goals and numerous plans that have helped us raise our children to adulthood. From these experiences, I have learned that no matter what stage of the parenting process you are in, it's helpful to develop a *Parenting Plan* that provides explicit guidance on how you will go about implementing and evaluating your parenting efforts. I have observed that, almost immediately after going through the process of developing a plan for parenting, parents tend to experience relief from anxiety. I have also observed that those who conscientiously implement these plans tend to do better and need less support than those who do not. Hence, I am convinced that every parent—especially those who are struggling to effectively parent teenagers—should develop and use a *Parenting Plan* that serves as a blueprint for their parenting labors.

This book formalized the process I recommend by describing, in some detail, how you can develop, implement, and evaluate parenting plans that are tailored to your family structure and needs. The book provides information and tools that will help you increase your parenting skills; systematically implement these skills; and set goals for your children that make explicit those things you want them to know, feel, and do when they become adults. It provides strategies for evaluating their performance to determine what your children know and do with regard to your family standards and outcome expectations. I have also provided you with guidance and tools that can be helpful in decreasing the likelihood of negative environmental influences and in increasing your likelihood of getting environmental support that reinforces your family standards and outcome expectations for each child.

The parenting methods and processes I have presented here are not theoretical fun and games. Rather, they are based on "what works" and "what is needed" to raise healthy, happy, and responsible children.

Specifically, this book provides information about how to effectively manage your family and train your children and includes the tools with which to do both—systematically. I also provide guidance on how to establish and communicate boundaries, how to contract for desired performance, how to motivate your children to do what they say they will do, how to evaluate performance, and when and how to obtain resources (books, training) or to call in a consultant (counselor, religious leader, teacher) to provide you with insight into difficult problems.

The book is divided into two sections. Section I, entitled *How to Develop and Implement an Effective Parenting Plan*, will help you 1) develop family goals and a goal statement, 2) decide which activities family members will engage in to achieve these goals, 3) set rules to support goals and activities, 4) justify rules, 5) select, assign, and administer appropriate consequences, 6) administer discipline appropriately, 7) motivate compliance with family rules, 8) contract for performance, 9) evaluate performance, and 10) develop and maintain a healthy relationship with each child.

The second section of this book is titled *Teaching to Assure Good* Health and Good Character. This section explains that a key parenting role is that of a teacher. And to be effective in this role, a parent must understand and apply correct principles in deciding what to teach and how to teach. This section provides you with 1) a list of possible topics that you may want cover, 2) a tool that can help you systematically decide which topics you will teach, 3) a description of a variety of teaching methods you can use, 4) information pertaining to developmental and psychological considerations in teaching, 5) guidance on how to develop a lesson plan around a particular topic, and 6) some sample lesson plans and lesson ideas that you can either teach or use as examples of how to prepare your own lesson plans. I have also provided a number of principles you should be familiar with when teaching.

The ideas in this book are grounded in a number of principles and assumptions about family structure and the role of parents. These are as follows:

- Parents are responsible for providing guidance and discipline for all children in the family.
- Parents will lead the family in formulating family goals that express the values, beliefs, attitudes, character traits, and behaviors the family will work toward adopting and maintaining.
- Parents will lead the family in planning and implementing activities designed to achieve family goals.
- Before family activities are implemented, parents will seek input from all family members.
- Parents will lead the family in setting rules that are designed to 1) help the family achieve specific goals by mandating

behaviors that contribute to these goals and by prohibiting behaviors that may prevent the goals from being achieved, and 2) support family activities by prescribing who will engage in each activity, and how and when the activities are to be performed.

- Parents will make final decisions about 1) the nature and scope of family activities, and 2) setting, modifying, and enforcing family rules.
- All rules must serve the purpose of supporting at least one family goal and/or activity.
- Before family rules and consequences are set, parents will seek input from all family members.
- Before family rules are implemented and enforced, all rules and consequences will be explained to all family members.
- When family rules are violated, parents will decide what consequences to administer. Consequences will be decided upon and administered within a specified number of hours of a rule infraction.
- All discipline will be administered in a manner that recognizes the shared right of every individual in the family to be treated kindly and respectfully. To this end, parents will use both natural and logical consequences when enforcing rules.
- All family members will understand that willingly participating in family activities and abiding by family rules will help a family achieve their goals.
- Parenting requires patience, long-suffering, kindness and, above all, love.

IT TAKES TIME TO GROW UP: WAIT AND SEE

The last principle listed above reminds parents that effective parenting requires patience. This is illustrated in a proverb found in most religious texts: "Raise up a child in the way he should go and, when he is old, he will not depart from the path." This proverb implies that the fruits of good parenting take time. Understanding this principle will help you have patience when your children make decisions that are contrary to what you teach them.

I once heard a story that has helped me remain patient when my life and my children do not always "turn out" the way I think they should. In other words, the story has helped me "lighten up" and enjoy the experience of parenthood.

After working in Beijing, China, for a period of time I decided to take a trip to the Great Wall. On the way to the Wall my driver suggested I stop in a small village and witness the making of different types of pottery. While looking over the pottery I remarked that I loved one of the vases that had the images of running horses painted on the outside. When the person who was showing me the piece learned that I was born in the "Year of the Horse," he told me a story that convinced me that I should purchase the vase as a reminder of the principle taught in the story.

Although the story may not be true, my guide told it as if it was and I am including it here because it illustrates my point. She said that in her village there lived a Zen master who loved horses. One day as he was meditating in the woods near the village he saw a horse grazing nearby. The master, knowing something about horses, was able to catch the animal and bring it back to the village. When he arrived at the village and corralled the horse, many villagers stopped by the master's house and remarked, "Master, you are very lucky, you captured a horse." In response the master would always say, "I will wait and see."

The next day the master's newly captured horse broke free and was lost again in the woods. When villagers found out, they stopped by the master's house and said, "Master, you are very unlucky, your horse has escaped." Again, the master said, "I will wait and see." The next day the master's son went out into the woods in search of the lost horse. After searching for a while he found the horse grazing in a meadow. The master's son was able to catch the horse and return it to his father, who then put the horse in a more secure corral. When the villagers heard the news they gathered at the master's home and said, "You are very lucky that your son was able to recapture the horse." As usual, the Zen master said, "I will wait and see."

The next day, the master's son was bucked off the horse when he tried to ride it. When he hit the ground, he broke his leg. When the villagers heard what happened, many visited the master's home and said he was unlucky because his son's leg was now broken. As always, the wise Zen master said, "I will wait and see."

The next day, a group of Chinese soldiers came to the village recruiting young men the age of the master's son to go to a serious battle across the Great Wall against the Mongolian army. That evening, after the dust settled, some villagers stopped by the master's house and said, "You are very lucky because your son broke his leg and did not have to go fight in the terrible battle." And as always, the master responded, "I will wait and see."

I have heard similar stories in many different countries. It is the story of "letting go" or embracing instead of fighting against the things that happen to us as a part of living. The Zen master understood this concept very well. He knew that declaring an event as lucky or unlucky was unwise because he also understood that we, as humans, do not have control over what happens in our day-to-day lives. Instead of fighting the realities of life, the master simply accepted the events of each day.

In spite of our best efforts, things happen. And fighting against, instead of learning to adapt to, these realities only brings us frustration. Embracing them, even when the events are very painful, allows us to feel peace in the midst of our sometimes chaotic lives. This is especially relevant in your role as parents where your only option is to teach your children correct principles and then stand back and hope they govern themselves in a way that serves their best interest.

SECTION I:

HOW TO DEVELOP AND IMPLEMENT AN EFFECTIVE PARENTING PLAN

CHAPTER 1

THE PARENTING LOGIC MODEL (PLM)

I n addition to the principles just described, I have developed a *Parenting Logic Model* that depicts how the strategies and tools in this book can be applied in the parenting process (see Figure 1). Moving from left to right, the model illustrates those problems among family members that cause stress on the family system. And, in every case, when there is stress the family attempts to alleviate the pain induced by this stress. The process of alleviating distress is called coping. Individuals and families cope in both healthy and unhealthy ways.

Healthy coping strengthens the family, while unhealthy coping weakens the family and its individual members. Accordingly, this book describes techniques that can be used to reduce problems, mitigate the distress caused by problems, and improve coping in response to stress. This process can be illustrated further by a number of examples. Before providing these examples, it is important to understand the concepts illustrated in Figure 1, namely, what we mean by problems, stress, and coping.

From a psychological perspective, problems are those things we register in our minds as discrepancies between the way things are and the way we would like them to be. Problems come in all sizes, from small to overwhelmingly large. For example, if we want our son to become a physician and he ends up dropping out of high school, we have a big problem. On the other hand, if we only expect our child to finish eighth grade and he drops out of high school after he has finished high school, we do not have a problem. In fact, we can be overjoyed because of this achievement.

With regard to stress that results from problems, as shown in the examples above, the family that expects a child to finish medical school experiences considerable distress when their child drops out of high school. Conversely, in the case of the child who finished high school when his family only expected him to finish eighth grade, there is very little if any stress placed on the family. Again, this is due to the fact that we only experience stress when there is a problem. And, as was mentioned above, problems are discrepancies between what we expect in life, and what we experience.

Ironically, we can reduce the number of problems in our life by lowering our expectations. This is not necessarily a good thing, but it is a fact. Another fact is that all people experience problems on a daily basis. We trip on bumps in the sidewalk, get caught in traffic jams, lose money in the stock market, get calls from teachers with concerns about how our children are doing in school, experience power outages in our homes, get laid off from work, slam fingers in a door, catch a cold, forget homework, etc. All of these problems result in stress. And, the more stress we experience in life, the more difficult it is to cope in healthy ways.

By coping in healthy ways, we take actions to alleviate stress that are legal, strengthen those who cope and others, and are based on sound, proven principles. Unhealthy coping includes actions that are illegal, not effective over the long run, and/or weaken the person who is coping or others. A rule of thumb here is that unhealthy coping is typically the path of least resistance and oftentimes makes the situation worse over time.

For example, drinking alcohol provides temporary relief from stress. However, because of the addictive properties of the drug and because simply taking a drink does not solve a problem, using alcohol to cope is not effective. This is also true with taking aggressive actions like screaming or hitting or passive actions like being too permissive. On either spectrum, hitting your children or letting your children do whatever they want can eliminate stress temporarily, but over the long run neither approach solves the problems that cause the stress. In fact, in parenting cases, both aggressive and passive approaches to resolving problems have proven ineffective and result in numerous negative consequences.

Now that you know something about the logic underpinning Figure 1, consider a few examples. Pretend that your 14-year-old daughter, Emily, has decided sneak out of the house late at night to meet some friends. Fortunately, Mom discovers Emily slipping back in the house at 5:00 a.m. Because it is not acceptable to Mom or Dad for Emily to sneak out at night, Mom, Dad, and Emily all have a problem.

At this point, the family is feeling stress. To alleviate the stress, Mom and Dad tell Emily she cannot go to a friend's sleepover birthday party as planned. Emily is crushed (more stress) so she starts criticizing both parents. Again, more stress on the family. In response to Emily's raging, Mom relents and says it's OK for Emily to go to the party if she agrees to be grounded the following weekend. Emily agrees, but Dad disagrees to this decision. Now Emily is feeling less stress, Mom is feeling less stress, and Dad is feeling more stress.

To alleviate his stress, Dad decides to scream at Mom for making a unilateral decision that went against their first decision to ground Emily. He explains that Emily has now learned that as long as she has complains loud enough, she can reduce her stress and delay or eliminate punishment for sneaking out of the house. Now Mom and Dad are feeling massive stress which, in turn, has a negative impact on their already fragile relationship. In fact, in this case the only person feeling minimal stress is Emily, who is now more confident in her ability to manipulate her parents to get what she wants.

Once again, let's look at Figure 1 as a way of analyzing this situation. Moving from left to right, the family was doing "OK" until Emily chose to disregard a family rule. Once Emily's infraction was discovered, Mom, Dad and Emily all had a problem. Because Mom and Dad did not agree about how to deal with the infraction, their first effort at coping was undermined when Mom unilaterally reversed the decision to punish Emily. This "unhealthy" coping response caused another problem for Dad, who felt stress and then coped in an unhealthy way by screaming at Mom. I have seen the long-term result from this type of coping with the family that raised Emily (her name has been changed to preserve confidentiality). It resulted in a divorce between Mom and Dad and may have contributed to Emily's death in a car accident when she was 17.

Another example with a better ending happened with a single mother, Susan, and her son, Philip (names are changed to preserve confidentiality). In this case, Susan came to me when Philip was 13 years old and explained that she was concerned that Philip was out of control at school. Her son was also starting to cause problems at home by hitting his younger sister and using profanity.

In our first session, I showed Susan the *Parenting Logic Model* and explained to her that we would work together to develop a plan to reduce the magnitude of the problems she was experiencing, relieve her stress, and cope in ways that would bring Philip back in line. Mom agreed, and the following week she came back to see me with a partially developed parenting plan. We worked together during this session and the following session to refine the plan and to prepare for a meeting with Philip.

In our fourth session, Philip was invited to join us to discuss the plan. To the credit of Susan, who was a very small and somewhat timid woman, she carefully laid out the plan in a way that Philip could not misunderstand the newly drafted family goals, rules, justifications for each rule, and both consequences and rewards that would come into play depending on whether or not Philip was compliant. Philip seemed to be compliant and respectful for the entire session and said he understood the plan and then signed it with the understanding that his signature meant he would comply with the family rules or experience the disciplinary measures laid out in the plan.

Two days after the session with Philip I was sitting across from a very frustrated Susan. She explained that Philip was worse than before and that he was unwilling to follow her consequences. As an aside, it is almost always the case the things get worse before they get better, especially with teenagers who are not accustomed to following parental rules. This was definitely the case with Philip who decided to declare all-out war on the new boundaries set down by his mother. Because the stakes were high, Susan and I decided to take things to the next level, which we had anticipated in the parenting plan. The plan stated that if Philip consistently disregarded family rules, Susan would contact the juvenile court system in her county and file an "Unruly Child Complaint."

Susan mustered up the courage to take this loving action to help her son. The next day (Wednesday), Susan filed the complaint, and the following Monday Philip was in front of a judge. The judge explained to Philip that he must obey his mother and then explained in explicit detail that if Philip did not comply, he would be in a heap of trouble. Philip was shaken to the core and decided that complying with his mom's plan was easier than experiencing the judge's consequences.

Although the end of Philip's story has not yet been written, his mom recently sent me a letter explaining that Philip had just finished the training required to become a firefighter in a large metropolitan fire department. She also explained that Philip had credited her willingness to stand up to him at age 13 and her consistency as a parent as important factors in his becoming a disciplined firefighter.

Once again, let's analyze the story of Susan and her son, Philip, against Figure 1 to see what happened. First, Philip started causing a number of problems in school and at home. Although this was not stressful for Philip, it caused his mom great distress. Consequently, she coped by contacting a therapist who had training in helping parents deal with difficult children. The counselor taught her how to develop a plan to deal with the problems and stress Philip was inflicting upon her and her daughter. Susan executed the plan, which initially caused more stress. Instead of giving up, a common coping mechanism for parents who do not know what to do, Susan coped in a healthy way again by showing up at my office.

Throughout our session, I helped Susan build the courage to take the plan to the next level—file an Unruly Child Complaint. Even though this action caused Susan even more stress because of her concerns about what this action would do to her relationship with her son, she went ahead as planned. Susan's coping decision to hold her son accountable—although it was an extremely difficult decision—turned out to be the best way to eliminate her stress and to resolve her problems over the long run. In fact, according to Philip, Susan's courage to hold him accountable motivated him to stay out of trouble, to graduate from high school, and to become a fireman.

My third example involves a young couple with two sons. The first time I met with these parents, they were in crisis. Their four-year-old son, Agusto, had just bitten another child in daycare, and the mother believed this was a sign that Agusto was possibly a sociopath (I am not joking). First, I helped the mother gain some perspective by convincing her that her son was too young to be branded with a label because of one action. After the mother agreed to quit yelling at her husband for agreeing with me, I was able to convince the couple to develop a plan that carefully outlined their expectations for their young son and the consequences they would administer if he did not comply. The finished plan was very brief and easy to understand and included many rewards for good behavior. Together, the parents and I explained the plan to Agusto and he excitedly agreed to participate. Two weeks later, the parents set up another session and spent the first several minutes saying how the plan had worked. They said Augusto loved the plan and had changed from being "out of control" at daycare to a model child. I do not know the end of this story because I never saw the family again. What I do know is that the parents felt great relief by systematically deciding how they were going to parent young Augusto.

These examples are but a sampling of the many challenges parents have brought to me. Because of these professional experiences, as well as my personal experience as a father of five grown children (including four sons), I feel confident in the effectiveness of the principles in this book. The remainder of the book explains in great detail how to develop and to apply effective parenting plans.

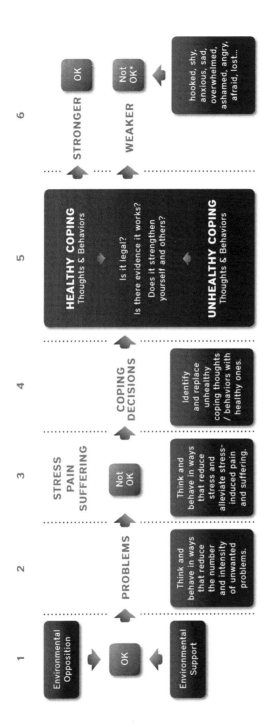

1
Environmental Opposition → OK ← Environmental Support

2
PROBLEMS
Think and behave in ways that reduce the number and intensity of unwanted problems.

3
STRESS PAIN SUFFERING
Not OK
Think and behave in ways that reduce stress and alleviate stress-induced pain and suffering.

4
COPING DECISIONS
Identify and replace unhealthy coping thoughts / behaviors with healthy ones.

5
HEALTHY COPING
Thoughts & Behaviors
Is it legal?
Is there evidence it works?
Does it strengthen yourself and others?
UNHEALTHY COPING
Thoughts & Behaviors

6
STRONGER — OK
WEAKER — Not OK*
hooked, shy, anxious, sad, overwhelmed, ashamed, angry, afraid, lost...

*Crisis Response: Call a friend, 911, a hotline, or your higher power; Meet with a therapist; Go to the nearest hospital emergency room; Take a cold shower; Attend a 12-step group

CHAPTER 2

DEVELOPING A FAMILY MANAGEMENT PLAN

A key parental role is to establish and maintain order in one's family. In fact, a defining characteristic of a functional family is the presence of order in the home; the opposite is often true in dysfunctional families, which are typically characterized by chaos and disorder. The parenting strategy outlined in this section of the book describes how you can develop a Family Management Plan and includes guidance on how to 1) develop a family identity statement and Mascot, i.e., "brand" your family, 2) develop family goals and a goal statement, 3) decide which activities family members will engage in to achieve these goals, 4) set rules to support goals and activities, 5) justify rules, 6) select, assign, and administer appropriate consequences, 7) administer discipline appropriately, 8) motivate compliance with family rules, 9) contract for performance, 10) evaluate performance, and 11) develop and maintain a healthy relationship with each child.

The first step in effectively managing your family is to put together a notebook that will eventually contain all those items that make up your *Family Management Plan*. When completed, this plan should contain your Family Identity Statement and Mascot, Family Goal Statement, a Family Calendar, your Family Policies and Procedures, and all the other items you will want to refer to as you attempt to implement your plan. This planning process and the resulting plans will equip you with the tools, knowledge, and skills to help you effectively fulfill your parenting roles.

CHAPTER 3

DEVELOPING A "FAMILY BRAND"

B randing is all about connecting. It's the connection between a person and something or someone else. Our senses affect our emotions, which in turn helps us create perceptions. These perceptions are important, as they are what ultimately affect our loyalty to that person or thing.

Think about the last experience you had at the DMV. You walk into the grey building, through the wobbly glass door that still has that black mystery residue on the hinges. You glance over the sea of people sitting in hard plastic chairs that look like they were thrown out of an old abandoned high school. You assume the dingy flickering lights are from the same school. You take your number and sit down in the third row of chairs like you are getting ready for a lecture (good thing you have your phone, so you can at least keep yourself preoccupied). You look around and see a faded picture of the Secretary of State on the wall, along with aged "Just say no!" posters. Your name is called and you prep yourself with what you know will be a "touchy" experience. You cautiously answer all questions. You have triple checked all your documents to make sure you have everything. You get your picture taken, holding your eyes open for dear life, anticipating that weird shadow behind your head. The picture comes out fine, considering your expectations were not that high anyway. You walk out and breathe a sigh of relief, hoping the next time will not be anytime soon.

Now, compare that with this experience. You walk up to a freshly painted building with fresh shrubbery and a manicured lawn. The solid framed door greets you with a smooth gliding motion as you enter. The lighting is soft, and the skylights provide

IDENTITY

What does your family "look" like? What symbol represents your family the best? Is it a literal symbol or an abstract shape that evokes some kind of emotion? Whatever it is, when people look at this symbol, they will think of you. Companies like Google only use typography for their brand identity, so yours does not have to have a graphic mark/symbol with it. What typeface will you use? What do you think of when you see Coca Cola's typeface versus Pepsi's? What about Home Depot vs. Lowes? Some typefaces take on a more playful look and feel, while others evoke a strong and powerful emotion. What does your family brand look like in a script font versus a font with very straight lines? If you do use a symbol of some kind in conjunction with typography, what does the symbol represent?

TAGLINE

Be creative with your family tagline. Taglines can send a succinct, but strong message about who you are and what your goals are as a family. They can also be quite memorable. Can you name the companies who own these taglines?

"Expect more. Pay less."
"What can brown do for you?"
"I'm lovin' it!"

If you said, Target, UPS, and McDonald's, then you are right on. Usually a tagline invokes some kind of emotion and creates a bond. Make your tagline as true as possible. If I walked into a Target store and "expected more," but paid a lot, then, well, I would feel betrayed as a customer, and my loyalty to that brand would be diminished.

COLOR PALETTE

Colors have a strong impact on our visual senses. We have had a favorite color since we were kids. I am sure it has changed over the years, but the point is, we have a special connection to color. Colors mean different things to different people. They take on different meanings for different cultures as well. Pick two or three main colors that represent your family. Here is a quick look at a few of the main colors and the feelings they typically represent.

Red is a color of energy, strength, power, and determination. It is also associated with love and passion. In many cultures, red indicates courage. *Example: Coke*

Orange is associated with joy and enthusiasm. It is also a color of creativity and determination. It is believed to stimulate mental activity and is highly accepted among young people. *Example: Harley Davidson*

Yellow is associated with intellect and energy. As you have noticed, taxis are usually painted a bright yellow because yellow is believed to be the "biggest" color and is very noticeable. *Example: Livestrong*

Green symbolizes growth, harmony, and freshness. Green suggests stability and endurance. A green light means "go," or "all is clear." *Example: Starbucks*

Blue is associated with depth and stability while symbolizing trust, wisdom, and truth. It is known to produce a calming effect and is seen as the most "sincere" color. *Example: IBM*

Purple makes people think of royalty and symbolizes power, nobility, and ambition. It is associated with wisdom, mystery, and magic. *Example: FedEx*

White means safety, goodness, and purity. It is usually associated with simplicity and perfection. *Example: Apple*

Black is a color of mystery. It hints at the unknown and is considered formal, elegant, and prestigious. There is a feeling of perspective and depth when black is used. *Example: Motorola*

PHOTOGRAPHY STYLE

When determining your photography style, you will really start to visualize what your brand "looks" like. If you were to describe your family to someone using pictures, what would you say? Are the images black and white or color? Are they images of people laughing or blurry people in motion? Each photo tells a small story of who you are.

Now that the foundation has been laid for your family brand, you can now move on to do any of the following activities that you feel would be fun or beneficial for your family. Use any or all of the elements above to create consistency and structure around your branded family materials.

WEB SITE

A website acts as a billboard or face of a company or organization. This is the place where they tell what they are all about. Your first encounter with any website will immediately cause an emotional reaction. What content do you want on the homepage of your family website? What overall message are you trying to convey? Develop "About Us," "Services," "News/Events," and "Contact" pages for your Web site. You may even want to link to a family blog, twitter, or Facebook account.

BROCHURE

Using the foundational elements, design a brochure. This should have the same look and feel as your website. What would the purpose of the brochure be?

POSTER

Imagine your family had their own movie, or they were planning a family reunion. What would the family poster look like? A poster should be visually striking and conceptual. People look at posters for a couple of seconds and move on. So, what one- to two-second story do you want to tell?

T-SHIRT

A T-shirt can be a fun way to unify your family. Companies use uniforms to say that they are all on the same team and that they are all unified with the same goals and mission. Your family T-shirt can be as simple or crazy as you want it to be. It does not have to have your family name on it, depending on your family's concept around the idea.

VIDEO

A family video will be a little more involved, but would be a great way to execute your family's overall concept and message. Is it a music video, a funny skit, mini-series, or a documentary? Who is the main character? What roles does everyone play? Not everyone needs to be in front of the camera. Some members of the family may like being "behind the scenes."

We do not all have family T-shirts and websites, but we do all display and market our family brand in a variety of ways. Creating and developing your family brand is something that will happen whether you like it or not.

Your strategy must be about personalization and customization. This makes your brand sincere and authentic. A well-designed strategy has personality and identifies us as sincere individuals. Your family brand will help set the tone for all that you do in developing your parenting plan.

CHAPTER 4
HOW TO DEVELOP A FAMILY GOAL STATEMENT

F amily goals are brief statements that specify the values, beliefs, attitudes, character traits, and behaviors you want your family and children to adopt and maintain. These goals should be future-oriented and challenging, but also specific, motivating, and achievable.

Each family goal is held up as a worthy ideal that family members are encouraged to work together to achieve and sustain. These ideals serve as standards against which you can evaluate how well you are doing as a family–and as individuals within the family.

As a way of placing emphasis on family goals, you can combine them into a single *Family Goal Statement* (FGS). A good FGS should list and briefly describe each important goal and some activities that family members will engage in to achieve this goal.

When you create your FGS, it is important that all family members participate in offering suggestions about the goal and what they can do to help achieve it. For example, if one of your family goals is for each family member to be happy, some viable suggestions are, "We will always try to be kind," or "Let's treat each other the way we want to be treated," or "We will obey all of our family rules." Anything else that the family agrees is a good goal can be added. Once you have formulated your FGS, it should be displayed in a prominent place in your home to remind each family member of the ideals represented by the Statement.

A sample FGS is provided here as Table 4.1. Use this example to guide you in developing your own FGS. First, list the values, beliefs, attitudes, character traits, and behaviors you want your family and children to work toward adopting and maintaining. For example, you may want your family members to be 1) happy, 2) fun-loving, 3) safe, 4) healthy, 5) talented, 6) humble, 7) modest, 8) respectful, 9) frugal, 10) environmentally sensitive, 11) orderly, 12) law-abiding, 13) moral, 14) ethical, 15) productive, 16) independent, 17) honest, 18) service-oriented, 19) socially adept, 20) trustworthy, 21) courageous, 22) responsible, 23) patient, 24) persistent, 25) self-confident, 26) assertive, 27) flexible, 28) competent, 29) forgiving, 30) hard working, and/or 31) spiritually balanced. If so, list and briefly describe each of these goals in column 1 of the worksheet.

After listing your goals, ask family members to offer suggestions on what they are willing to do, individually and collectively, to help achieve each goal. List these suggestions in column 2 of the worksheet.

TABLE 4.1: SAMPLE FAMILY GOAL STATEMENT

FAMILY GOAL	WHAT FAMILY MEMBERS WILL DO TO HELP ACHIEVE THE GOAL?
1. Our family members will be safe.	We will not give our names or address to strangers on the Internet.
	We will wear seatbelts every time we ride in an automobile.
2. Our family will work toward and cooperate in keeping our house and yards in order.	We will do all of our assigned chores in a timely manner.
3. Our family will be supportive of other family members.	When possible, we will attend the activities of other family members, such as concerts, soccer games, plays, and award ceremonies.
	We will give encouragement to other family members when they are trying to overcome problems.
4. Our family will communicate in ways that strengthen family relationships	We will learn to avoid using "bad conversation habits" like name-calling.
	We will listen to and validate the opinions and feelings of other family members.

Once you have developed and prominently displayed the goals outlined in your FGS, you should refer to them often. In fact, each goal can serve as a point of discussion in the lessons you will teach your children (see Sample Lesson Plans, Chapter 19).

To encourage our children to adopt the goals listed on our FGS, my wife and I typically set aside time in our weekly family meeting to discuss a particular goal. For example, one of the goals included in our FGS is to "show support for other family members." When discussing this goal during one of our family meetings, my wife and I explained to our children that we would like them to show support for their siblings by attending their athletic events, plays, and other activities. We further reinforced this standard by setting aside time in our weekly family meeting to discuss the upcoming activities of each family member and, in turn, encouraging all family members to attend. This type of advance notice provides our older children, who have many activities of their own, the opportunity to plan to attend their siblings' activities.

Before embarking on managing and training your children, you need to begin (or continue, whichever the case), a process of bringing your attitudes and actions in line with the goals outlined in your goal statement. What your children observe in your behavioral patterns is what you will more than likely observe in their attitudes and actions when they become adults. That is, children have the unique ability to see past our words and focus on our attitudes and behaviors. Although there are no perfect parents, the more closely you align your behaviors with your FGS, the more likely it is that you will be able to persuade your children to do the same.

CHAPTER 5

THE PLANNING AND ORGANIZING GUIDE

I t is important to systematically plan the activities you will use to achieve your family goals. Some of the most important reasons for conscientiously planning and organizing your family affairs are to 1) set directions, 2) identify resources needed to get where you want to go, 3) examine alternative courses of action, and 4) develop an action plan with specific assignments. The process I am recommending entails planning in advance of an activity who will do what, when, where, and how often.

Before beginning the planning process, decide what aspects of your family life you want to plan. At a minimum, I recommend that you formulate plans that address such things as 1) a weekly family meeting, 2) maintaining the household, 3) work, 4) meal prepara- tion, 5) finances, 6) education, 7) recreation, 8) communication, 9) conflict resolution, and 10) personal development.

The bottom line when considering what to plan is simple: Whatever aspects of your family life you hope to organize and manage efficiently should be carefully planned.

The tool I recommend for planning is called the *Planning and Organizing Guide* (POG). Instructions for using the POG are provided in Table 5.1 (Tables 5.2 and 5.3 provide examples). This guide is used to generate what I call *Family Policies and Procedures*. All plans generated using this guide should be included in your *Family Manage- ment Plan*.

TABLE 5.1: PLANNING AND ORGANIZING GUIDE (POG)

1. List all the things you want to plan. For example, household maintenance, recreation, and family boundaries. Each of these items will become a separate section in your Plan.
2. Complete a separate POG form for each of the items listed. Don't hesitate to modify this form and create your own, for you may have an approach that works better for your specific circumstances. The important thing is to systematically plan and follow through.
   A. Write the item you want to plan in row 1.
   B. Under column 1, list all those things you want to plan under the area you are focused on at this time.
   C. In column 2, describe what you want done in connection with each item in column 1.
   D. In column 3, describe who will do how much of what, how often, by when, and where to accomplish what you want done.
   E. In column 4, record when and how you will follow up to determine if the specific actions items in column 3 have been accomplished.
   F. Record special instructions in the bottom row of the chart.

AREA OF FOCUS:

List Things You Want to Plan under this Area	Describe What You Want Done	Describe Who Will Do How Much of What, by When, and Where	Record When, How and How Often Will Follow Up on Action Items

SPECIAL INSTRUCTIONS:

TABLE 5.2: SAMPLE FAMILY PLAN #1 USING THE POG

AREA OF FOCUS: FAMILY ACTIVITIES

List Things You Want to Plan under this Area	Describe What You Want Done	Describe Who Will Do How Much of What, by When, and Where	Record When, How and How Often Will Follow Up on Action Items
Monthly Family Activity	Present ideas for family activity to family members at weekly family meeting. After activity has been selected, determine what needs to be done to plan the activity and make assignments to appropriate family members.	Dad will present four different options for a family activity to all family members at the next family meeting. Family members will select an option and Dad will make assignments, as he deems appropriate. Dad will follow up to determine whether assignments are accomplished and make family members aware of what they need to do to prepare for the activity.	Dad will follow up at each of the next four family meetings (more often, if necessary) to determine whether assignments have been made and to inform family members of what they need to do to prepare for the activity

**With advance notice, family members will clear their schedules so they can attend the activity.

I suggest that a specific time be set aside for developing your family plans. It is ideal to retreat to a place where you can focus your attention on developing and refining the plan. The plan should be considered a work in progress because you will need to modify it as circumstances change and as you gain experience in raising your children.

Shortly after the plan is initially developed, and every time it is modified, you should seek feedback on the plan before it is fully implemented. You can get feedback in a number of ways. For example, you can ask experienced parents for suggestions. You should also seek your children's input before the plan is finalized. Let your children know that you value their comments unless, of course, they are expressed in a disrespectful manner. Allow your children to express themselves openly, even on non-negotiable items. Record their suggestions and feedback.

Once you have received feedback on the plan, meet again with your spouse and consider how to use the feedback to improve the plan. After the plan has been revised, call a meeting with your children and go over the plan you want to implement. Let the children know when the plan will be implemented. Also, let them know that the plan is a living document that will be revisited on a regularly scheduled basis (i.e., every four to six months). Schedule the next time you will take comments on the plan. Each time you solicit comments on the plan, record the comments and meet in private with your spouse to use the feedback you get to improve the plan.

TABLE 5.3: SAMPLE FAMILY PLAN #2 USING THE POG

AREA OF FOCUS: CHILDREN'S CHORES

List Things You Want to Plan under this Area	Describe What You Want Done	Describe Who Will Do How Much of What, by When, and Where	Record When, How and How Often Will Follow Up on Action Items
Wash dinner dishes	Take clean dishes out of dishwasher and put them away. Clean off table, rinse off all dirty dishes, put dishes in dish-washer, put soap in dishwasher, and turn on dishwasher.	Dad on Saturday and Sunday, Josh on Monday and Tuesday, Nicholes on Wednesday and Thursday, Mom on Friday	Every evening, before 9 p.m., all dishes must be done or you get an additional day added to your dish schedule.
Vacuum main floor	Vacuum all carpets on the main floor.	Josh will do this every Saturday morning.	Mom or Dad will follow up to determine completeness before 10 a.m. on Saturday.
Vacuum upstairs	Vacuum all carpets upstairs.	Nicholes will do this every Saturday morning.	Dad will follow up to determine whether the task is completed on time.

Mow and trim lawn	Mow the front, back, and side yards. Use a bag on mower and place clippings in mulch pile. Trim around the entire house, including the deck and sidewalks.	Josh will do this every Saturday (unless it rains, in which case the first dry day after Sunday) from May 1 through October 1. Other times as needed.	Mom or Dad will check to see if the lawn is mowed. The lawn must be mowed before leaving 10:00 a.m. on Saturday.
Clean upstairs bathrooms	Use cleaning solution to clean the tub and toilet. Use separate clean rag on each. Use a third rag to clean sink and mirrors. Mop the tile floors with floor-cleaning solution.	Jordan will do this every Satur-day morning.	This bathroom must be cleaned before 10 a.m. every Saturday morning. Mom and Dad will fol-low up. You may not leave the house or have friends over until this chore is completed.

**Note: If for some reason you can't do your assigned chores, please make arrange-ments with another family member to do them for you.

Do not change the plan in the presence of your children. Always retreat with your spouse when you are thinking about modifications. Otherwise, you run the risk of the children manipulating the plan by playing you against your spouse. Place the plan in a colorful binder in a location where everyone in the family has ready access to it.

Organizing naturally follows planning, because planning involves designing and making provisions for accomplishing all the things you plan to do. In short, it involves making sure that you and your children have ready access to all the information, resources, equipment, outside services, and so on, required to implement and achieve your goals. For example, if you want your children to perform specific chores, you should make sure that they have ready access to the tools they need to carry out their assigned responsibilities. If you expect them to study for one hour every day, you should provide a place in your home where they can study without being disturbed. Column 3 in the POG (decide who will do how much, of what, by when, where, and how often) is designed to help you organize the family goals you have planned to accomplish.

Admittedly, formulating a *Family Management Plan* is no easy task. It requires a considerable investment of time and, when two parents are involved, it can become a real struggle that requires considerable negotiation. However, an important side benefit comes from the process of planning with your spouse. This process, more often than not, requires considerable self-disclosure, negotiation, and compromise. If you and your spouse approach this process seriously, by investing the time and energy required to "put your ducks in a row" (beyond the ears of your children), your family management (parenting) efforts will become more and more refined, effective, and efficient over time.

Finally, make sure you plan for the unexpected. Be flexible and, where it is appropriate, build in contingency plans. For example, what happens when the child who is responsible for doing the dishes is sick? Are the dishes left undone? Is the child required to do the dishes on an assigned night if he or she has a highly communicable disease? Obviously, there needs to be some back-up plans to cover contingencies. These contingency plans should be recorded under the action section of your FMP.

CHAPTER 6

SETTING AND JUSTIFYING FAMILY RULES

F amily rules help the family achieve family goals by 1) mandating behaviors that contribute to the goals, and by 2) prohibiting behaviors that may prevent the goals from being achieved. For example, if a family goal is to do well in school, a family rule designed to support this goal might state, "All students in the family will complete all homework assignments before watching television."

Rules can also contribute to family activities by prescribing who will engage in each activity, and how, when, where, and how often such activities are to be performed. For example, a rule about doing the dishes might state, "On Monday, Wednesday, and Friday evening, Jordan will rinse and place all dinner dishes in the dishwasher before 9 p.m."

You should link all family rules to family goals and activities. This will help you justify the rule and ensure that all rules contribute to your efforts to establish and maintain a healthy, functional family.

My wife and I have established many rules over the years. Some of our rules are as follows:

- You will do all your assigned chores in a timely manner.
- You will not use the property of others without first getting their permission.
- You will attend all family meetings (unless you have been excused in advance).
- You will show support for family members by attending their activities (when possible).
- You will not use vulgar or profane words.
- You will always tell the truth.
- You will do your homework before you watch television or play video games.

- You will apologize and make amends for personal mistakes that impact others.
- You will resolve conflicts peacefully, without raising your voice or hitting.
- You will abstain from alcohol and other drugs.
- While living at home, you will attend Church/Synagogue/ Mosque every week, unless you have a good reason not to.
- You will not stay out past your curfew.
- Before leaving the house, you will always let your parents know where you plan to go, what you plan to do, and when you plan to be home.
- You will treat your family and friends with kindness and respect.
- When we have trouble communicating, we will use structured communication.

The *Family Rule Development Guide* that follows will guide you through the process of setting, justifying, and deciding on consequences for all family rules. First, list all rules in column 1. In column 2, provide a justification for each rule listed in the first column. Typically, the justification should explain how the rule helps to 1) achieve one or more family goals and/or 2) ensure that one or more family activities are carried out as planned. In column 3, you will list consequences for not abiding by a family rule (see Tables 6.1 and 6.2).

TABLE 6.1: FAMILY RULE DEVELOPMENT GUIDE		
Family Rule Must support at least one family goal.	**Justification for Rule** Consider benefits of rule and how it supports goals/activities.	**Consequence(s)** Apply discipline via natural or logical consequences.

When setting rules, you want to identify some basic core rules and then support these core rules by establishing several small preventive rules. For example: If you have a core rule stating, "Don't use drugs," then you will want to set some preventive rules such as WHO your teen may associate with, WHAT types of activities are allowed, WHERE your teen is allowed to go, and WHEN your teen may go–as well as WHEN he or she is expected to return. It would be foolish to believe that your teen could hang out at the wrong places or associate with drug-using friends and remain drug-free. When you create preventive rules alongside your main core rules, you provide your teen with the greatest amount of protection. You also become involved, so that you can be aware of problems early and resolve them before they become overwhelming.

TABLE 6.2: SAMPLE FAMILY RULE DEVELOPMENT GUIDE		
Family Rule Must support at least one family goal.	**Justification for Rule** Consider benefits of rule and how it supports goals/activities.	**Consequence(s)** Apply discipline via natural or logical consequences.
When we are having difficulty communicating, we'll use *Structured Communication* (see explanation in Chapter 11) .	The main benefit to using structured communication is that it provides a safe way to communicate clearly and effectively without fear.	Poor communication, including nonproductive discussions, unresolved issues, frequent conflict, hard feelings, etc.
You may not hit another member of the family.	Hitting can cause both physical and emotional injuries. It can also damage relationships.	Consequences, depending on culprit's age and the severity of the infraction, may include a verbal reprimand, a required apology, and/or a loss of privileges.
Do all your chores in a timely manner.	Doing your part reduces the burden on family members and ensures that the house and yard stay in order.	Verbal reprimand, extra service hours, and/or loss of privileges
When conflict is escalating, you should call a *Time-Out* and try communicating again, using structured communication, or agree to talk about the issue later, at a specified time.	This rule serves to protect and enhance relationships by counteracting the negative escalation that is so destructive to close relationships. Conversations escalating into fights always result in hurt feelings and block overall communication.	An apology and the requirement to have a 15-minute *Positive Communication Rehearsal* using structured communication

Before leaving the house, you will always let your parents know where you plan to go, what you plan to do, and when you plan to return.	By informing your parents of your intended plans, they can warn you of possible hazards, reach you in case of an emergency or unforeseen event, know where to look for you in case you are stranded, etc.	Loss of privileges and/or extra service hours
We will look for the positive traits in other family member's attitude, actions, and appearance, and compliment them accordingly.	Accentuating the positive in other family members strengthens relationships and increases feelings of self-worth.	Some natural consequences that result from accentuating the positive when interacting with family members are 1) increased self-esteem and feelings of being appreciated, 2) better relationships among family members, and 3) decreased conflict and improved communication. Negative consequences imposed by parents may include an apology by the offenders and *Positive Communication Rehearsal.*
We will have a weekly "family meeting."	This rule ensures that you will set aside a time, on a regularly scheduled basis, to deal with important issues and problems. This is a tangible way to place a high priority on your family.	Natural consequences are that activities are not planned, appointments are missed, family members don't communicate, etc.

Once rules have been established in draft form, you may want to share them with your children. After receiving feedback, revise your rules accordingly and produce a final set of rules, justifications, and consequences. Share this final set of rules with your children and let them know that the rules will be enforced until further notice. Revisit the rules on a periodic basis to revise, if necessary, those rules that are flawed (e.g., impractical, unenforceable, too lenient, not specific).

CHAPTER 7

HOW TO ENFORCE FAMILY RULES

When children willfully disobey family rules and are resistant to counsel, it will be necessary to enforce the previously set consequence. The process of enforcing consequences in response to misbehavior is called discipline. *Discipline* is a form of teaching and correcting that is designed to motivate compliance with family rules. It should be based on a contingency relationship similar to the one described above, where set consequences are administered when a specific rule is violated. The underlying principle is based on the assumption that an undesired behavior will decrease if followed by an unpleasant consequence.

Unpleasant consequences that can be applied to administer discipline include 1) "grounding" or restricting movement (such as in a time-out), 2) removing privileges (such as having friends over or using the phone), 3) restricting the use of personal items or removing them altogether (such as favorite clothes or stereo), 4) corrective verbal chastisement, 5) extra service hours, or 6) spankings. The primary concern when selecting negative consequences is to identify those consequences that produce the degree of unpleasantness required to cause the child to stop misbehaving.

A general principle to remember when selecting consequences is that "the discipline should be proportional to the offense" and should be administered in appropriate, loving ways. When discipline is out of proportion to the infraction—and/or when it is administered in a harsh fashion—it can do more harm than good. I am also convinced that insufficient discipline can result in negative consequences. The secret is balance and patience. Neither will prevail, however, unless you have planned, in advance of the infraction, such things as what the discipline will be, in what instances it will be administered, who will administer it, under what circumstances, how often, and at what level of intensity.

There are two broad categories of consequences that allow a young person to experience the actual result of his or her own behavior. I have labeled there natural and logical consequences.

Natural consequences are the direct result of a young person's behavior. Examples include getting injured when jumping off a high ledge, getting bitten when petting an unfamiliar dog, or getting arrested for driving over the speed limit.

Logical consequences are established by the parents and are the direct and logical consequence of the transgression; consequences should not be arbitrarily imposed. Examples include losing the privilege to use the family car after getting a speeding ticket, being restricted from using the computer after visiting pornography sites, having to pay for a broken window after hitting a ball into the window, or receiving extra chores after not completing regularly assigned tasks.

What follows is a list of natural and logical consequences for use when dealing with noncompliance with family rules. These consequences are not in any particular order and should be applied with justice in mind. That is, "The punishment should always fit the crime."

Grounding: The reason I start with grounding is because it is one of the most popular tactics used by parents. In my opinion, it is also the most misused tool in the toolbox because it often comes out of a parent's mouth as a spontaneous response to many different misbehaviors. And, parents often apply this consequence without thinking through the implications grounding has on them. This is why grounding is typically modified after tempers cool. And, when it is modified, the children learn the worst possible lesson from their parents—that parents are not consistent and that discipline is not predictable.

I do believe grounding is a great tool if it is used correctly and in the context of a thought-out parenting plan. So how is grounding carried out correctly?

First, you must realize that when you ground a child, you ground a parent. If you really mean your child is going to stay home all weekend and not do anything except sit on his or her bed and contemplate misbehavior, a responsible adult will need to stay home and observe the punishment as it takes place.

A much better approach is to assign chores to the child who is on restriction. And, once the extra chores are assigned, explain to the child that the restriction is not over until all the chores are completed. This approach has many advantages: 1) the family benefits from the work that is getting done by the child/teen on restriction, 2) it is easy to monitor and observe the beginning and end of the restriction, and 3) it allows the offender to control how long he or she is on restriction. It is also good practice for "unruly children" who, later on, may experience community service by court order.

Once again, grounding and all of the disciplinary measures that follow should be carried out within the guidelines of your parenting plan. This way you and your child know the rules and the consequences that follow noncompliance.

Apology: Apologies are one way that individuals can help repair the damage done in a conflict characterized by bad conversational habits. The child/teen may be asked to apologize to the offended party (e.g., parent or sibling) in writing or in person. It is important that the offending child/teen accept blame for the incident and demonstrate authentic regret when offering the apology, or neither party will be satisfied with the outcome.

Behavioral Contract: The child/teen and parent work out a written agreement that outlines specific positive behaviors that the child/teen is to engage in (or specific negative behaviors that he or she is to avoid), the privileges or rewards that the child/teen will earn for complying with the behavioral contract, and the terms by which the child/teen is to earn the rewards (e.g., making his or her bed for three consecutive days). Likewise, the consequences of not complying with the specific requirements outlined in the contract should be recorded in the contract.

Over-correction: The child/teen is required to repetitively practice a skill that will "replace" or improve upon an inappropriate or problematic behavior. For example, a child/teen who does several other things before carrying out a parent's request to go to his room and do his homework may have to stay in after school one day and take several "practice" trips to his room, where he gets out his books, reviews his assignments, and begins doing his homework. In this example, the parent might accompany the child/teen to monitor how promptly he walks to his room and to give the child/teen feedback about how much the target behavior has improved. Another example of over-correction is to assign additional chores to a child/teen who has neglected assigned chores.

Verbal Reprimand: In the typical reprimand, the parent approaches the child/teen, states that the child/teen is misbehaving, and instructs the child/teen to stop misbehaving immediately. Reprimands should refer to the undesirable behavior and not slander the child's character. They should be kept short to avoid arguments with the child/teen. Reprimands should be used sparingly, as child/teen may become defiant if repeatedly confronted by an angry parent. If used too frequently and indiscriminately, verbal reprimands lose their effectiveness and become reinforcers of undesired behavior because they grant attention to the child. Verbal reprimands given by parents during time-outs are a major cause of reduced effectiveness of this form of discipline.

Redirection: The parent interrupts problem behavior by calling on the child/teen to answer a question, assigning him or her a task to carry out, or otherwise refocusing the child's attention.

Reasoning, or Away-from-the-Moment Discussions: In general, it is more effective to anticipate and prevent undesirable behavior than to punish it. "Away from the moment" refers to dealing with difficult behavior not in the heat of the moment, but instead, in advance or away from the actual misbehavior. An away-from-the-moment discussion provides the parent with opportunities to teach what behavior is acceptable. It has the potential to serve as a very useful tool to prevent undesirable behavior, because it allows the parent to teach the child/teen the desirable behavior in anticipation. For example, if you child/teen misbehaves in a public setting you can choose to address your concern in a private setting at home instead of making a scene at the site of the infraction.

Positive Communication Rehearsal: When individuals are having difficulty communicating or are not willing to communicate in healthy ways (i.e., they have one or more conversational bad habits), they can be required to practice positive communication using a structured communication method. The rules are as follows:

1. One person speaks at a time. This person is designated as the *sender*. This person expresses thoughts, concerns, and desires in a respectful manner to another person who is designated as the *receiver*.
2. The *receiver* listens carefully to what is being said and, after the *sender* has spoken, simply paraphrases what the *sender* has said. That is, the *receiver* repeats back, in his or her own words, what the *sender* said as a way to demonstrate to the *sender* that he or she is listening. A simple format that can be followed by the listener is—
    i.   What I heard you say is (paraphrase what the sender said).
    ii. Is that right?
    iii. Is there more?
3. After the *sender* feels like the *receiver* understands what he or she has to say, the roles reverse. That is, the *sender* becomes the *receiver*, and the *receiver* begins to speak.

Promise: The parent approaches the misbehaving child/teen and informs that he or she has behaved inappropriately. The parent asks the child/teen to state an appropriate alternative behavior that he or she should have followed. The parent then requests that the child/teen promise the parent (verbally or in writing) that he or she will not engage in this misbehavior again.

Reflective Essay: The child/teen is required to write and submit to the parent a brief composition after displaying ill behavior. At minimum, the composition would state (1) what problem behavior the child/teen displayed, (2) how the child/teen could have acted in an alternative, more acceptable manner, and (3) a promise from the child/teen to show appropriate behaviors in similar situations in the future.

*Note: Some parents use a pre-printed, structured questionnaire containing these three items for the child/teen to complete.

Response Cost: Usually, response cost programs first award a child/teen a certain number of tokens, with no conditions attached. Throughout the monitoring period, the child/teen has a token withdrawn whenever he or she displays a behavior that is inappropriate. (These behaviors usually have been agreed upon in advance.) The child/teen is permitted to "cash in" any points that he or she still retains at the end of the monitoring period or may be allowed to "bank" the points toward a future reward or privilege.

Restitution: If a child/teen breaks or loses another family member's property, he or she would be required to both apologize for the act and replace the property. If the property is irreplaceable, the child/teen should, at a minimum, pay some compensation for what is lost. The point here is that the child/teen engages in an activity that actually or symbolically restores the environment, setting, or social situation that his or her misbehavior has damaged.

Rewarding Alternative (Positive) Behaviors: The parent "catches" the child/teen engaging in appropriate behavior and provides positive attention or incentives during these times. The same positive attention or consequences are withheld during times when the child/teen misbehaves.

Rules Review: The parent approaches the misbehaving child/teen and 1) has him or her read off the posted family rules, 2) asks the child/teen which of those rules his or her current behavior is violating, and 3) has the child/teen state what positive behavior he or she will engage in instead.

Time-Out Suspension or Removal of Privileges: For young children, time-out usually involves removing parental attention and praise (ignoring) or placing the child in a chair for a specified time with no adult interaction. For older children and adolescents, this disciplinary measure usually involves removing privileges or denying participation in activities. To be effective, this strategy requires that a valued privilege is removed.

As with grounding, several aspects of time-out must be considered to ensure effectiveness. When time-out is first implemented, it usually will result in increased negative behavior by the child, who will test the new limits with a display of emotional behavior, such as a temper tantrum. The parent who accepts this normal reaction and does not respond to the child's behavior will find that outbursts become less frequent and that the targeted undesirable behavior diminishes or disappears. When time-out is used appropriately, the child's feelings are neither persistent nor damaging to self-esteem, despite the intensity of the reaction. However, if the parent engages in verbal or physical interaction with the child during the time-out, the emotional outburst, as well as the behavior originally targeted, will not only persist, but may in fact worsen. Second, time-out is often not effective immediately, although it is highly effective as a long-term strategy. Third, it is often difficult emotionally for a parent to ignore the child during periods of increased negative behavior or when the child begins pleading and bargaining for time-outs to end. The inability of parents to deal with their own distress during a time-out is one of the most common reasons for its failure.

Some specific suggestions for effective time-outs include:
- Pick the right place. Be sure the time-out location does not have built-in rewards. The TV should not be on during time-out.
- Time-out should last one minute per year of the child's age, to a maximum of five minutes.
- Prepare the child by helping him or her connect the behavior with the time-out.
- Introduce time-out by 24 months of age.
- Keep time-out quiet. It is not the time for teaching or preaching; save the lesson for later.
- Use time-out for the older child to reflect on his or her misbehavior.
- The parent should be the timekeeper.
- Clear the air afterwards. That is, after time-out is over, it is over, and a new activity can then begin.

Loss of Privileges: The child/teen is informed in advance that he or she can access a series of privileges (e.g., use the family car, watch TV, play a video game, spend the night with a friend) if his or her behavior remains appropriate. The parent instructs the child/teen about what kind and intensity of problem behavior may result in the loss of privileges, and for how long. After this introductory phase, the parent withdraws privileges as agreed upon whenever the child/teen misbehaves.

Disciplinary Spanking: The use of disciplinary spanking as the dominant method of teaching acceptable behavior should be discouraged. By definition, disciplinary spanking refers to spanking that is physically non-injurious, administered with an open hand to the buttocks, and intended to modify behavior. All efforts to discipline should be made with other techniques. Situations where disciplinary spanking is considered by some to be an option are rare and are limited to instances when the child has placed himself or herself in danger. However, some argue that a firm restraint and "No!" would be equally effective.

Over the years, there has been a raging debate among parenting experts with regard to whether or not parents should administer physical discipline. However, this debate has greatly subsided, and it appears that the vast majority of experts in this area counsel against physical discipline, noting that although hitting a child can have an impact on the child's behavior, in the end, it is simply not effective.

Much of the evidence in this area comes from animal training. Time and again, it has been proven that beating animals (as opposed to reinforcing desired behaviors) is simply not effective. Everyone has seen animals that are carefully nurtured and willing to perform almost any trick for a reward. I have noticed this response in the horses I own. The ones that were trained without beatings are cooperative and sound. The two I have that were trained the "old-fashioned way," with a whip and intimidation, are distrustful and occasionally dangerous. The point is, beating animals or children to get them to go along with your will is simply not effective. Hence, when asked my opinion, I encourage parents to err on the side of not hitting their children. Once again, after raising five children of our own, my wife and I agree that physical discipline should be used with great discretion, if at all.

Without exception, inappropriate and harmful means of discipline include the following: slapping, kicking, punching, arm twisting, shaking, pinching, ear pulling, jabbing, shoving, choking, beating, or delivery of repeated demoralizing blows to the unruly child. These techniques fall outside the range of "disciplinary spanking."

Another cardinal rule of discipline is worth mentioning here. If at all possible, DO NOT discipline when you are angry. Cool off before setting the terms of discipline. This provides you the time required to get all the facts and to consider the motives of the child who committed the infraction. If you ignore this advice, you will more likely than not find yourself overreacting and punishing rather than disciplining. In such cases, it is not uncommon to assign discipline and/or punishment that "does not fit the crime." If you do assign discipline that does not fit the infraction (typically, this happens when we judge out of anger), it is okay to go back to the child and revise the discipline.

Just as being too harsh in your approach to discipline is ineffective and counterproductive, so is being inconsistent and/or too lenient in terms of discipline. Even though parents want to be loved by their children, they should realize from the outset that parenting should never be considered a popularity contest. This is particularly true when the two contestants are the parents. Children will, by nature, manipulate any differences of opinion they detect between their parents and will uphold the more lenient parent as the one they "love the most."

It is true that a parent can gain the loyalty of one or more of the children by indulging and giving broad license to them. However, this strategy often causes disharmony with their spouse who, in some cases, may overcompensate what he or she perceives to be insufficient discipline by applying excessive discipline. This can, in turn, strengthen the allegiance of the child to the more permissive parent.

Although being the more popular parent has its rewards, it also has its downside. For example, the more permissive parent is constantly being asked permission and is subject to pressure tactics designed to get him or her to give permission. Moreover, the disharmony between the spouses created by the lenience of one partner can have a negative impact on the entire family.

To avoid manipulation and all the other consequences that come with an uneven plan for administering discipline, it is important that both parents agree about what the rules are and what disciplines will be administered when the rules have been violated. This requires planning, cooperation, and "buy-in" from both partners.

Another thing to remember when you are assigning discipline is that when you punish or restrict your child, you also restrict yourself to the extent that you must follow up to make sure that your child complies with the discipline. This is why it is so important that before either parent administers discipline, both parents discuss the discipline and how it will be carried out. When you discipline without your spouse's consent or "buy in," you can place an undue and unexpected burden on your spouse without proper notice. For example, if your wife is a stay-at-home mom, it may be easy for you to ground your children for a week because all you have to do is pronounce the words while your wife has to literally "stay-at-home" with them for a week. This is not a problem if your wife agrees to suffer the discipline along with your child. But to arbitrarily assign your wife to policing the home for a week is not fair or considerate.

As was mentioned above, a better alternative to grounding or other forms of restriction is to assign what I call *extra service*. Again, there are a number of advantages to assigning extra service. It is easier to monitor a child who has assigned tasks to perform, for the period of restriction is determined by how long it takes the child to perform the extra service. The child can be taught that the service is a form of restitution for whatever he or she has done wrong. This form of discipline requires forethought and planning, but is well worth the effort.

In summary, to discipline appropriately, you should first be explicit about what you expect of your children and, while remaining calm, hold them accountable when they do not comply. Once again, this technique requires some advanced planning so you and your spouse know what expectations you hold for your children (see the *Family Rule Development Guide*).

CHAPTER 8

MOTIVATING AND REWARDING DESIRABLE BEHAVIORS

Without motivation to carry out the *Family Management Plan*, those who have been assigned various responsibilities will probably not do all they are assigned to do. If this is the case, your best intentions to bring order to the family will remain just that, good intentions. A great plan is of little value if it is not implemented faithfully. For this to happen, those who have been assigned specific responsibilities must perform their duties. And, to ensure success in managing those who are assigned to implement the plan, you must learn to motivate them.

Fortunately, researchers have discovered a number of principles that can be applied to increase a child's motivation. The overriding principle that I apply in my efforts to motivate my children is called the *Premack Principle*. This principle is that any *high probability behavior* (things your kids really like to do) can be used to reinforce a *low probability behavior* (things they do not like to do). I have found that this principle has a number of practical advantages that have helped us motivate our children/teenagers to carry out their responsibilities. For example, if I want to motivate our child to do something he or she is not likely to do (a low probability behavior), like sweep the garage or wash the dishes, I must make performing a high probability behavior, like going out with friends, contingent (dependent) upon the low probability. That is, "Yes, you can play video games if you first [the contingency] make your bed and feed the dog."

In psychological literature, the Premack Principle is applied in a motivational learning theory called Operant Conditioning. This theory relies on the principles of contingency, reinforcement, and shaping in the process of motivating compliance with recommended or desired actions.

The principle of *contingency* suggests that, as is implied by our above example, your child is more likely to carry out his or her responsibilities when the things he or she likes to do are dependent (contingent) upon the performance of a responsibility like mowing the lawn or folding and putting away clothes. (Note how I used this principle of consequences in our Parent/Child Contract). For example: "Son, you may NOT go out with your friends on Friday [a high probability behavior] unless you mow the lawn on Thursday [a low probability behavior]."

On a day-to-day basis, many consequences are contingent upon behavior. For example, getting paid is contingent upon working, physical alertness is contingent upon the amount of rest you get, knowledge is dependent upon the amount of training and experience a person has, and so on. The concept of contingency is important here because it is used in connection with reinforcement (or reinforcers) to motivate the performance of assigned duties.

Reinforcement is a principle that refers to the presentation of an event or stimuli which, in turn, results in an increase in the frequency of a desired behavior. There are two types of reinforcement: positive and negative.

A *positive reinforcer* is distinguished by its specific effect on the desired behavior. If you give your child a reinforcer—like money—in connection with a behavior you want him or her to engage in—like washing the car—and your child's car-washing behavior increases, then the money is a positive reinforcer. Hence, the defining characteristic of a positive reinforcer is its ability to increase the desired behavior it follows, like vacuuming, dusting, homework, taking telephone messages, and so on.

The more common term "reward" is often used synonymously with positive reinforcers. However, in the strictest sense, a reward is not a positive reinforcer unless it actually increases the frequency of a desired behavior. If, for example, you reward your daughter with money for making her bed on Tuesday morning and she chooses not to make her bed on Wednesday morning, the monetary reward was not a positive reinforcer.

Some examples of reinforcers I have used to successfully increase desired behaviors include the following: 1) verbal praise, 2) the privilege of spending the night, 3) money, 4) toys, 5) eating out at a favorite restaurant, 6) ice cream, 7) stickers, 8) check marks on a chore chart, 9) concert tickets, 10) the car, and 11) poker chips that can be cashed in for money.

From the family management perspective, the principle of positive reinforcement carries a strong message: If positive reinforcers can be implemented, children can be motivated to perform desirable, low probability behaviors. And the stronger the reinforcer, the more motivation the child will have. Therefore, the very key to motivating our children to carry out their responsibilities lies in our ability to accurately identify strong reinforcers for each child.

Once you have identified your children's individual reinforcers, it becomes possible to use them as a basis for motivating desired performance. Formulating a *reinforcement schedule* that is designed to apply these principles can help with this process.

A reinforcement schedule can either be continuous or intermittent in nature. *Continuous reinforcement* requires reinforcing an event every time it occurs. In contrast, *intermittent reinforcement* requires reinforcing only after your child has done what you want him or her to do a number of times. For example, paying a child five dollars every time he or she washes the car is continuous reinforcement, but paying the child a weekly allowance if (the contingency) he or she completes all assigned chores is an intermittent reinforcer.

In most instances, continuous and intermittent reinforcement schedules produce important differences in the performance of desired behavior. For example, during the initial stages of adopting an assigned behavior, continuous reinforcement is more likely to motivate early performance. For a number of reasons, intermittent reinforcement schedules are preferred, particularly for maintaining your child's behavior.

Many times, a desired behavior cannot be motivated by reinforcing a single response. This is due to a number of factors, such as the complexity of the behavior or the age and knowledge of the child. In such instances, I suggest the use of another operant conditioning principle called *shaping*.

Shaping a desired behavior involves reinforcing small steps or approximations toward a desired action rather than reinforcing only the desired response. The final desired behavior is eventually achieved through the reinforcement of successful approximations, which resemble the final response. For example, if your child receives a failing grade in advanced algebra, she may need to improve her study habits before her grades increase. Therefore, in your attempt to raise your child's grade (your goal), you could set up a contingency schedule that reinforces a higher grade at the end of the semester ($5 for a C, $10 for a B, and $15 dollars for an A). Likewise, you can set up a shaping schedule composed of small steps to help ensure that the goal is reached, such as reading a book on how to study, studying for one hour every day after school, and/or working on a computer program that teaches advanced algebra.

Another principle that pertains to motivation is termed self-fulfilling prophecy, or the *Pygmalion Effect*. In the mid 1960s, Drs. Rosenthal and Jacobson told the teachers of elementary age students that, based on the results of an achievement test, some of the students in each class were "likely to show unusual intellectual gains in the year ahead." In fact, there was no measurable difference between the test scores of the students who the researchers labeled "superior" students and those of the other children. As Rosenthal and Jacobson anticipated, the students who had been labeled "potential achievers" showed significant gains in IQ. This finding was attributed to the notion that teachers expected more of the students labeled as achievers. The researchers referred to this phenomenon as the Pygmalion Effect because "they felt that teachers' expectations had influenced the students to become intelligent in the same way that the expectations of the mythical Greek sculptor Pygmalion had caused a statue he had carved to become endowed with life (Rosenthal and Jacobson, *Pygmalion in the Classroom*, 1968)."

The link between this concept and parenting is that if parents communicate high expectations to a child that he or she can make good decisions, do well in school, be hardworking, and so on, the likelihood that the child will develop these positive traits will increase. The classic movie *My Fair Lady* illustrates the Pygmalion effect. Two different individuals in the movie treat a lowly flower girl, Eliza, differently. The effect of this treatment is revealed when the flower girl says to one of the characters in the movie, "I shall always be a flower girl to Professor Higgins because he always treats me as a flower girl, and always will, but I know I can be a lady to you, because you treat me as a lady, and always will."

It is true that our children come to us with many strengths and shortcomings. I am convinced that if I place less emphasis on their weaknesses and magnify their strengths in our conversations and in the way I treat them, eventually their strengths will overshadow their shortcomings.

Some related strategies (Based on Operant Conditioning) that have been used to discourage negative behavior and to reinforce positive behavior are allowances and token reward systems.

Allowance: I recommend that each child receive a weekly allowance that is composed of both earned and unearned portions. Receiving the earned portion is contingent upon complying with some prescribed routine (i.e., a chore chart) that has been agreed upon in advance. Meanwhile, the unearned portion is an amount of money that the child receives irrespective of performance. Consistently receiving an unearned amount of money reminds the child that much of what they get from parents is unearned. By paying the unearned portion, the parents also ensure that the child will consistently receive money that can be used to cover some ongoing expenses. Making a portion of the allowance contingent upon performance teaches a work ethic and can be used as an incentive for healthy attitudes and actions.

Token Reward System: An effective strategy that employs frequent reinforcement as a means of motivation is the use of a token economy. This involves determining, in advance, what types of behaviors and attitudes will be reinforced, as well as the level of reinforcement. Every time a pre-designated behavior is performed by a child, that behavior is reinforced by a chip that can be turned in for a reward. Conversely, when the child disobeys a rule, a designated number of chips is forfeited. Table 8.1 is an example of a reward system that can be used to motivate certain family chores.

TABLE 8.1: CHORE AND ACTIVITY CHART

CHORE/ACTIVITY	MON	TUES	WED	THR	FRI	SAT	SUN
Make Bed	W	W	W	W	W	W	NC
Clean Room	W	W	W	W	W	W	NC
Feed Harley the Dog	W	W	W	W	W	W	NC
Take Trash & Recycle Bins to Street	W						
Return Recycle Bin to Garage	W						
Sweep Kitchen	Whenever Mom or Dad Ask (R)						
Load or Unload Dishwasher	Whenever Mom or Dad Ask (R)						
Vacuum Upstairs Hall						R	
Sweep Garage						B	
Extra Chores	Whenever Mom or Dad Ask (W)						

Directions: You must do your chores to receive an allowance. Every chore is worth a certain amount of money. You will be paid in chips during the week. You can turn these chips in for money on Saturdays. The type of chips you will receive for each chore is designated by W, R, or B. The chip values are: W=white chip, worth $0.10; R=red chip, worth $0.25; B=blue chip, worth $0.50, and NC=no chip. Whenever you do a chore, either collect a chip from Mom or Dad at bedtime, or circle the chore on the chart and collect your chips all at once on Saturday.

Index Card Reinforcement System: Another version of the token system that has been used in a variety of inpatient and outpatient settings is called the *index card reinforcement system*. This system involves writing reinforcers on 3x5 cards and then assigning behaviors to a certain number of cards. Once again, the defining characteristic of a reinforcer is its ability to increase the desired behavior it follows, like doing homework, obeying curfews, feeding the dog, making a bed, and so on.

A tool my wife and I have used to implement this system can be seen in Table 8.2 below. To implement the system, we simply transferred all of our family rules into column 1 of this table. After we listed our rules, we assigned a certain number of cards to each rule by recording a number in column 2. The number of cards was based on how important we, the parents, considered the rule to be. For example, we assigned more cards to a rule that has to do with safety, like "do not give your home address to strangers you meet on the Internet," and fewer cards to rules having to do with things like homework or making a bed before school.

Although it is more time consuming, we listed in column 3 the privileges our children were restricted from until they completed the tasks listed. It should be noted here that the more a child acts out, the more specific you will need to be in articulating and enforcing consequences. This principle is discussed in more detail in the next chapter.

TABLE 8.2: INDEX CARD REINFORCER CHART		
Family Rules (Transfer All Family Rules to this Column)	Number of Reinforcer Cards (List the Number of Cards You Want to Assign to this Rule)	Lose All Privileges until Tasks on the Reinforcer Cards Are Completed (Optional but Helpful for Parents with Bad Memories)

Directions: When you break a family rule listed in column 1, you will be required to complete the assigned number of cards listed in column 2. In column 3, we have listed the activities you will not be able to participate in until you complete your reinforcer cards.

CHAPTER 9

CONTRACTING FOR PERFORMANCE

When you are raising a young person with chronic behavior problems, you may want to consider contracting for desired performance. Although this technique can require considerable time, it works when less formal interventions fail.

You can prepare a behavioral contract by 1) specifying all the expectations you have for your child, such as time to get out of bed in the morning, chores, restricted places or friends, and curfew; 2) stipulating the consequences of not complying with the contract; 3) informing your child of the contract and negotiating the terms of the contract, where appropriate; 4) signing the contract with your child; 5) following up to ensure that the terms of the contract are complied with; and when they are not, 6) enforcing the consequences specified in the contract. The following table will help guide you in developing a Parent/Child contract.

TABLE 9.1: PARENT/CHILD CONTRACT

CONTRACT BETWEEN (NAMES OF PARENTS AND CHILD):

Things I Will or Will Not Do	Consequences if I Do Comply	Consequences if I Do NOT Comply

I agree to comply with all that is described in this contract. I also understand that if I do not comply with those things described in column 1, I will incur the negative consequences stated in column 3.

CHILD'S SIGNATURE:

These contracts may seem rigid, but in many cases they are very helpful in bringing order to the life a young person who is out of control. If you are having great difficulty communicating with your child, you may want to enlist the help of a professional (counselor, psychologist) in negotiating these contracts. I have provided you with an example of such a contract in Tables 9.1 and 9.2.

TABLE 9.2: SAMPLE PARENT/CHILD CONTRACT

CONTRACT BETWEEN (NAMES OF PARENTS AND CHILD):

Things I Will or Will Not Do	Consequences if I Do Comply	Consequences if I Do NOT Comply
I will not stay out past 9 p.m. on a school night or 11:30 p.m. on a weekend.	I can leave the house in the evenings without asking permission.	I will be required to come home one hour earlier for one week.
Before I leave the house, I will tell my parents where I intend to go and what I intend to do.	I can leave the house in the evenings without asking permission.	I will ask permission every time I want to leave the house. I will not be allowed to use the car.
When I go out on weekends, I will not go anyplace where alcohol is served, nor will I associate with friends who encourage me to drink.	I can leave the house in the evenings without asking permission.	I will be placed on restriction for two weeks during which I won't be able to go out on weeknights or weekends.

I agree to comply with all that is described in this contract. I also understand that if I do not comply with those things described in column 1, I will incur the negative consequences stated in column 3.

CHILD'S SIGNATURE:

If, in spite of your best efforts to persuade your child to comply with your family rules, your son or daughter continues to disregard your parental authority, you may want to seek help from your local Juvenile Justice department. Typically, to get their assistance you will need to file an "Unruly Child" complaint. In the state that I am most familiar with (Georgia), the definition of an unruly child is *a child who is habitually and without justification truant from school; is habitually disobedient of the reasonable lawful commands of his or her parent(s), guardian(s), or other custodian(s) and is ungovernable; has committed an offense only applicable to a child; deserts his or her home; wanders or loiters about the streets between the hours of 12 midnight and 5 a.m.; patronizes bars; possesses alcoholic beverages; disobeys the terms of supervision contained in a court order; commits a delinquent act, and is in need of supervision, treatment, or rehabilitation.*

If your child fits this definition, I strongly urge you to consider contacting your local Department of Juvenile Justice. This may seem like a harsh approach to parenting. However, my experience tells me that in some cases, it is the only way to get a young person's attention and send the message that he or she is required by law to accept reasonable parental supervision and direction. In so doing, both parents must agree to, and be willing to see through, the process.

Of course, your child will complain profusely, not realizing that you are taking these measures to save his or her future, and even his or her life in many cases. Such complaints should be ignored, just as your child has ignored your parental demands to comply with family rules. My advice to parents who have trouble ignoring their child's unfounded pleas for mercy and who tend to give in to their child's demands is to say things like, "toughen up" or "buy a helmet." This is meant to communicate the message that parenting can be very difficult at times, and rather than walking away from the challenge, you need to take whatever measures are appropriate to bring things under control with the understanding that the sooner you intervene, the better.

CHAPTER 10

EVALUATING PERFORMANCE

E valuating performance is key to the success of your *Family Management Plan* because a perfectly designed and administered plan is a waste of time and energy if it is not implemented as planned. To do this requires some understanding of performance standards and how they apply to the process of evaluating your child's performance.

Performance standards are those expectations you have concerning how you want your child to perform a task, such as study for a test, wash the car, mow the lawn, practice the piano, or wash the dishes. When you evaluate a child's performance, you compare what you want or expect the performance to be (the performance standard) to what you observe it to be. If there is a considerable discrepancy between what you want and what you get in the way of performance, then your child is underperforming. However, this may or may not be the child's fault. For example, if you consistently set a bad example by not performing at the level you expect your children to perform at (i.e., you tell them to make their beds and you never make yours), it is likely that they will perform at the level of your example rather than performing in accordance with your stated expectations.

Poor performance can also result when you do not clearly describe, and in most cases demonstrate, what you expect your child to do. In such cases, you are mostly to blame for poor performance because your children should not be expected to read your thoughts and guess what you want them to do. They should know precisely what you expect.

Another cause of poor performance can be partly due to not being organized. For example, if you ask your 10-year-old son to mow the lawn and you provide him with an old decrepit lawn mower that he must push up and down a steep hill, it is likely that you will get a relatively poor performance–*if* your son performs at all. Once again you are to blame, because if you want good results, you need to provide your children with the resources they need to perform at a high level.

If, however, you make a practice to explicitly state, even write down, what you want in the way of performance, demonstrate how you want your child to perform, and provide your child what he or she needs to perform at the expected level, then the child must shoulder the responsibility for poor performance. In other words, only after you have taken all excuses away from your child by carefully explaining and demonstrating what you want done, and providing the equipment or environment in which to do it, can you legitimately hold the child accountable for not doing what he or she is capable of doing (assuming the child has the necessary intellect and strength to do what you want done). The key here is to explicitly state your expectations so your child has no uncertainty about what you want him or her to accomplish.

Another key in evaluating performance is to discipline yourself to follow up and both 1) evaluate performance by comparing what you expect to what you want, and 2) if there is a discrepancy, hold the child accountable and require him or her to do better next time until the task is performed correctly. Letting your child off the hook when he or she is capable of performing at a level that meets your expectations only teaches your child the bad habit of underperforming. This habit is difficult to overcome and can carry into adulthood.

Follow up and evaluation are integral parts of any family intervention, policy, or procedure that you may develop or implement as a result of reading this book. Consequently, rather than developing a separate evaluation tool here, I have incorporated these concepts into the various tools I have recommended that you use.

professional calf-roper on the rodeo circuit. All of this came out of a concerted effort to help our son. This experience has reinforced our belief that it is much easier to parent and teach a child when we are playing and working together. This idea is summed up by a billboard sign I once saw: "Children spell love, T I M E." When you invest time in your child, you will develop a relationship that will carry you through the difficult times.

To further supplement the relationships among family members, we have set aside one night a week as family night. On this night (held on Mondays), we all get together and talk, go bowling, ride horses or four-wheelers, go to nice restaurants, etc. We also plan to start these evenings with a formal discussion on a topic of interest. We have discussed things like table manners, how to prevent electrocution (do not leave our hairdryer plugged in and laying in the sink), drugs and alcohol, dates, music, and sex, to name a few. Once again, the goal of these meetings is to bring the family together to build our relationships and to provide a forum for my wife and I to pass along what we want our children to know and do to become healthy, happy, responsible adults.

We also believe that family vacations are a must in building family relationships. They give the family time to regroup without friends around. As with every other family activity, we feel like vacations should be planned in advance with input from all family members. This is especially important if you have teenagers.

The implications of Dr. Roger's teachings are that to be an effective parent, you must develop a good, healthy relationship with each child. Although this takes time and effort (like playing basketball or going fishing or taking a walk), the payoff is great in the teen years when your child's outlook on life begins to change.

As was discussed at the beginning of this section, a defining characteristic of a functional family is the presence of order in the home. The parenting strategy outlined in this section has provided you with ideas about how to develop a *Family Parenting Plan* that can be used to 1) develop a family identity statement and mascot, i.e., "brand" your family, 2) develop family goals and a goal statement, 3) decide which activities family members will engage in to achieve these goals, 4) set rules to support goals and activities, 5) justify rules, 6) select, assign, and administer appropriate consequences, 7) administer discipline appropriately, 8) motivate compliance with family rules, 9) contract for performance, 10) evaluate performance, and 11) develop and maintain a healthy relationship with each child. The next section will discuss principles that must be understood to effectively implement your *Family Management Plan*.

CHAPTER 12

PRINCIPLES OF GOOD INTERPERSONAL COMMUNICATION

Interpersonal communication is key to every aspect of developing, implementing, and evaluating an effective parenting plan. In fact, lack of communication and miscommunication are the hallmarks of a dysfunctional family. In view of the need to communicate effectively, your *Family Management Plan* should include guidelines for communication. For example, the FMP could address communication as an area of focus by developing plans for achieving consistent family communication and effective interpersonal communication. These goals could be accomplished by holding regularly scheduled family meetings and by teaching each family member the principles of good interpersonal communication, respectively.

Regularly scheduled family meetings can provide you with the family time required to develop and implement your FMP. For example, we have used these meetings as a time to resolve family conflicts, plan vacations, obtain feedback on our FMP, and instruct our children on a number of topics, ranging from personal hygiene to drug use. Perhaps the most important reason for holding these meetings on a consistent basis is to demonstrate to your children that you value family communication. Some guidelines for holding family councils are as follows:

1. Meet on a regularly scheduled basis.
2. Plan ahead by setting an agenda.
3. Establish ground rules to ensure order, such as "only one person will speak at a time" and "all comments, including negative comments, must be made in a respectful manner."

4. Decisions that are made can be voted on with the parents reserving the right to veto decisions that they feel are not in the best interest of the family or a particular family member.
5. Begin the session on a positive note.
6. Strive to include everyone by giving each participant a meaningful assignment.
7. Although parents should always preside, children should have the opportunity to participate and should be allowed to offer suggestions that are taken seriously.
8. Do not allow the meeting to degenerate into a gripe session. However, each member of the family should be free to openly and respectfully express his or her feelings on the issues being considered by the council.
9. Practice good communication skills during the council. These skills are described in some detail in a later chapter.

Be patient if your meeting gets off track, particularly if members of your family are communicating in positive ways. Since the very essence of a family meeting is family communication, I consider our meeting a success even if nothing else is accomplished besides good communication between family members.

As was mentioned above, a good way to keep your family meetings on track is to set an agenda. Some agenda items that we have included on our family council agenda are as follows:

1. Review calendar and *Activity Request Forms* and correlate upcoming activities.
2. Plan weekly family activity.
3. Assign or clarify chores, such as clean the main-level or upstairs bathroom; mow or trim yard, hoe the garden, weed the yard; wash breakfast, lunch, or dinner dishes; wash doors, woodwork, walls, or windows; dust furniture; take out trash; vacuum downstairs, main level, or upstairs; shop for groceries; sweep the garage and sidewalks; etc.
4. Review a "family standard" or expectations concerning family rules.
5. Communicate and discuss a new or existing item in the *Family Management Plan*.

6. Teach a lesson/principle from one of the seven topic areas included in the next section of the book.
7. Memorize and discuss an inspirational thought.
8. View a video or listen to a training tape.
9. Read a book.
10. Serve refreshments.

*One thing you may want to consider adding to your family meeting is the idea of an *Activity Request Form*, a very useful tool for improving communication through advanced planning. At one point in the process of raising our children, my wife and I were experiencing a lot of last-minute requests to do things like go to the movies, go skating, spend the night, and so on. This was frustrating because if we did not give our children permission, they would get upset. If we did give into their pleading, we typically had to make adjustments in our own schedule to accommodate their last-minute request. In other words, their last-minute emergency requests turned into our problem.

To overcome this problem, I devised an *Activity Request Form* (see Table 6), which I presented at our weekly family meeting. This planning form, when used on a consistent basis, helps alleviate last-minute requests and places the burden of planning on our children instead of on the parents. It also teaches children to think and plan ahead, which often results in a much better activity. This is not to say that it is wrong to be spontaneous. It can be great fun to plan an activity at the last minute. However, if you want to simplify your life and bring order to your family, giving in to last-minute requests should be the exception rather than the rule.

TABLE 12.1: ACTIVITY REQUEST FORM

Please be prepared to answer the following questions when you want to participate in an activity with your friends. To increase the likelihood that we (your parents) will give our consent to your requests, please 1) ask permission at least two days in advance of the activity, 2) earn the money required to cover the costs, and 3) have all of your daily/weekly chores done. Also, please be prepared to describe the following:
• The activity you want to attend or participate in,
• The cost of the activity,
• Who will pay the cost,
• Where (all the places you plan to go to) the activity will take place,
• When you plan to leave the house,
• Who will be at the activity (adults and youth),
• When you plan to return home,
• Who will provide transportation to and from the activity, and
• Whether or not you have done all your chores this week.

Oftentimes, communication needs to be one-on-one to be most effective. This is particularly true when discussing sensitive matters or administering discipline. It is helpful to schedule personal interviews with your children on a regular basis. For example, have a standing date with your son or daughter every week or every month (e.g., every Wednesday or the first Sunday of every month). This can be a time when you develop a close relationship with your child by sharing intimate details about problems, concerns, hopes, aspirations, and so on. If you establish this tradition early on in your child's life, it will become a habit.

To further improve communication, you should take the time to learn about your child's interests and those things he or she is most passionate about. Does your child like music? If yes, learn what types of music he or she prefers, and who the artists are, including such things as their hit records and how they became popular. Along the same lines, most teenagers like movies. If you learn something about their favorite actors, you are in a position to carry on a conversation that will interest them.

You may ask yourself, "Why would I want to learn about these things, especially if I don't like the types of music or movies my children like?" At such times, remember this is not about you and your interests. Rather, it is about discovering what your child is interested in and making a point to talk about these things, so he or she is willing and interested in talking to you.

Communication requires a sense of timing. For example, many young people are not ready to talk about "the events of the day" right after school. When our four older children were in high school, they often brought friends over on weekends and we all talked late into the night. Many times those late night talks were very revealing with regard to the concerns and ambitions of our teenagers and their friends. Why? Because that is when our kids and their friends wanted to talk and so we (typically my wife) met them on their own terms.

Another good way to encourage communication is to take walks with your children. Our family lives near a park where we like to take a daily 3-mile walk around the 1.5-mile walking trail. These walks were especially helpful for one of our teenagers, who would tend to vent his issues and concerns about life for the first 1.5 miles, and then laugh and talk about all sorts of things during the second half of the walk. I learned to simply listen and withhold advice and judgment during lap one, and then enjoy the conversation the second time around.

Our third son loves to fish. So how might I engage him in a conversation? If you guessed that I ask him a fishing related question, you are right. Another way to get his undivided attention is to ask him if he wants to rent a boat and go fishing.

When giving advice to our children, I attempt to accentuate the positive. For example, tell them what they should do instead of what they should not do. Say, for example, "Wear your helmet each time you ride your horse." Do not say, "Do not ride your horse without a safety helmet."

When I feel a need to give advice to one of our older children, it is typically given sparingly and usually takes the form of questions such as, "Have you thought about this, that, or the other?" or "Have you tried this, or that alternative?" I have found that communication usually shuts down when I get into a "You should do this" or "You should do that" mode. Hence, I use "shoulds" sparingly.

Sharing feelings, especially negative emotions such as anger, sorrow, embarrassment, and fear, can be difficult at times. There is a lot of "emotional baggage" that goes along with negative feelings. When your children become teenagers, they will know how to effectively exploit your weaknesses and hit your "hot buttons," so to speak. This is why it is so important to understand and apply sound communication principles when relating to your children.

When you or your children are having great difficulty communicating about a particular topic, as evidenced by such things as shouting, I recommend two strategies to help you in the process: *time-out* and *structured communication*. Time-out, as the name suggests, simply involves agreeing to separate for a period of time until things cool down. This is very useful when communication begins to escalate. However, this strategy must be agreed upon in advance as a step toward resolving conflict. That is, you must teach your children, and agree as a family, that whenever communication begins to get out of hand, anyone in the family can request a time-out and everyone who is involved in the communication will agree to separate for a period time.

I call the second strategy for facilitating communication structured communication because limits are set on how and when those engaged in a discussion can communicate. There are a number of advantages to agreeing to engage in structured communication. First, it provides boundaries that, if honored, prevent communication from getting out of hand. Perhaps the most important benefit of structured communication is that it teaches those who participate in the process how to listen.

Engaging in structured communication is simple and effective. First, those engaging in the communication agree in advance that they will follow the rules. As I pointed out in Chapter 6, these rules are as follows:

1. One person speaks at a time. This person is designated as the *sender*. This person expresses thoughts, concerns, and desires in a respectful manner to another person who is designated as the *receiver*.
2. The *receiver* listens carefully to what is being said and, after the *sender* has spoken, simply paraphrases what the *sender*

has said. That is, the *receiver* repeats back, in his or her own words, what the *sender* said as a way to demonstrate to the *sender* that he or she is listening. A simple format that can be followed by the listener is—

    i. What I hear you say is (paraphrase what the sender said).

    ii. Is that right?

    iii. Is there more?

3. After the *sender* feels like the *receiver* understands what he or she has to say, the roles reverse. That is, the *sender* becomes the *receiver*, and the *receiver* begins to speak.

Once again, I highly recommend adding this type of structure to communication when you are struggling to do it well. You will discover that the reason this approach is so effective is because it strikes the root cause of why people do not communicate, which is the inability or unwillingness to listen carefully to what the other person has to say. Structured communication forces the receiver to listen to and understand the sender before speaking.

CHAPTER 13

MESSAGE MAPPING: A STRATEGY FOR COMMUNICATING AROUND HIGH CONCERN ISSUES

When people are stressed or upset, they often have difficulty speaking, hearing, understanding, and remembering information.
*- **Vincent Covello***

As a psychotherapist I am oftentimes asked by parents to help them through very difficult situations. And, more often than not, these situations involve teenagers.

A tool that has helped parents communicate more effectively about high concern issues like drugs, dating, sex, AIDS, abortion, legal issues and any other potentially volatile or sensitive topics is called *Message Mapping*. This is a structured process that generates a "message map" that can be used by parents in preparing for and engaging in important conversations with their children.

A message map is a roadmap for displaying detailed, hierarchically organized responses to anticipated questions or concerns. It is a visual aid that provides, at a glance, the parent's messages for high concern or controversial issues.

Developing and using message maps can achieve several important parenting communication goals, including 1) anticipating your children's questions and concerns around difficult issues before these issues are raised, 2) organizing your thinking and developing prepared messages in response to anticipated questions and concerns, 3) developing supporting facts and proofs for each key message, and 4) promoting open dialogue about messages both inside and outside your family.

The process parents use to generate message maps can be as important as the end product. Message mapping exercises often reveal fundamentally differing viewpoints between parents in how each would respond to the same question, issue, or concern. If these differing viewpoints are not clarified and agreed upon by both parents in advance of dealing with difficult parenting issues, parents can send conflicting messages. The savvy teenager will see these inconsistencies and manipulate them toward his or her own goals, which are oftentimes not in the teen's best interest. This is why parents should sit down together to develop message maps around important issues that relate to family values, identity, and personal habits.

Several steps are involved in constructing a message map. The first step is to identify a complete list of your children's questions and concerns. The fact is, most questions that will be raised related to a controversy or concern can be anticipated. Here are some anticipated questions: "Hey Dad, what's wrong with using marijuana or drinking alcohol?" "Hey Mom, why can't I date college guys? I *am* sixteen." "What's wrong with having sex with my boyfriend?" "Why can't I go to an overnight party at the lake?" "Why can't I spend the night at my girlfriend's house?"

Most concerns expressed by young people and their peers are associated with a limited number of underlying issues about relationships with their peers, dating, sex, substance use, academics, religion, health and safety, appearance, money, equity/fairness, honesty and trust, parental control, and accountability.

The second step in message map construction is to organize your thinking and develop prepared messages in response to anticipated questions and concerns. That is, develop three key messages in response to each of the questions you have listed in the first step. Key messages are typically developed through brainstorming with your spouse or with a therapist or pastor or grandparent. The brainstorming session produces a message narrative, which in turn is reduced to key messages that can be entered on the message map.

Key message construction is based on principles derived from one of the main theories of communication—*mental noise theory*. According to Dr Vincent Covello, a renowned expert in message mapping exercises, mental noise theory states that when people (your kids) are upset, they often have difficulty hearing, understanding, and remembering information. Mental noise can reduce a person's ability to process information by over 80 percent. The challenge for parents, therefore, is 1) to overcome the barriers that mental noise creates, 2) to produce accurate messages, and 3) to achieve maximum communication effectiveness within the constraints posed by mental noise. Parents must strive for conciseness, brevity, and clarity.

Solutions to mental noise theory that guide key message development specifically, and message mapping generally, include:

- Developing a limited number of key messages: ideally three key messages or one key message with three parts for each underlying concern or specific question (conciseness);
- Keeping individual key messages brief: less than 9 words for each key message and/or less than 27 words for the entire set of three key messages (brevity).
- Developing messages that are clearly understood by your children: typically at the grade readability level that is most appropriate for your child (clarity).

Additional solutions include:

- Placing messages within a message set so that the most important messages occupy the first and last positions.
- Developing key messages that cite credible third parties.
- Using graphics and other visual aids to enhance key messages. For example, use graphic images or videos of the effects of tobacco on the body and/or injuries sustained by drunk drivers.
- Balancing negative key messages with positive, constructive, or solution-oriented key messages. This is based on the 1N=3P rule. This communication rule is based on research revealing that for every negative interaction between two people, it takes at least three positive interactions to restore the relationship to where it was before the negative transaction occurred.
- Avoiding unnecessary uses of the words no, not, never, nothing, none.

The third step in message map construction is to develop supporting facts and proofs for each key message. The same principles that guide key message construction should guide the development of supporting information.

The fourth step in the process is to prepare to use the map. This means you should study and practice the use of each message map before delivering the messages to your children.

In addition to the four steps and principles just described, it is important to keep this adage in mind during the communication process: "People want to know you care before they care what you know." To account for this principle, you will note in the following examples that a message map includes a space for an opening statement. This statement should express a sense of caring, such as, "I would first like to say that I value you very much and want the best for you now and in the future." This type of introduction to any conversation around a sensitive topic tends to increase the likelihood that the listener (your son or daughter) will actually pay attention to what you have to say.

Examples of this four-step process can be seen in Tables 13.1 and 13.2. I have added background statements to each example so that you will have some context for the map and how it was used.

TABLE 13.1: MESSAGE MAP ON A QUESTION ABOUT SEX

BACKGROUND (THIS SECTION IS NOT INCLUDED IN A MESSAGE MAP. I HAVE INCLUDED IT TO HELP SET THE CONTEXT FOR THIS MAP): THIS IS A MAP USED BY A SUNDAY SCHOOL TEACHER WHO WAS CHALLENGED WITH THE FOLLOWING QUESTION AND STATEMENT.

Question: What's wrong with having sex before marriage? All of the kids at school have sex.

Opening Statement: During our lesson last week, Laura asked a very serious question. It's such an important question I said I would take time to answer it in this week's lesson. Before I begin, let me say that the reason I took extra time to prepare my response is because I care deeply about each of you and believe you deserve a well-thought-out answer.

Message 1: There are many advantages to delaying sex.	Message 2: Engaging in sex at a young age can have serious irreversible consequences.	Message 3: There are many things you can do on a date besides engage in sexual activity.
Supporting Fact 1A: Dating without sex gives you time to learn how to discern sexual motives and avoid sexual exploitation.	Supporting Fact 2A: Most relationships between teenagers don't last, whereas most serious consequences do last.	Supporting Fact 3A: Dating is fun and is designed to allow you time to get to know people of the opposite sex, such as how they think and what they like to do.
Supporting Fact 1B: Delaying sex can reduce the likelihood that you will get a sexually transmitted disease or AIDS.	Supporting Fact 2B: Sexually transmitted diseases (STDs) like herpes, venereal warts and HIV are incurable.	Supporting Fact 3B: Instead of worrying about the pressure of sex on a date, consider these activities: exercising together (riding bikes or jogging), going to a concert,, going to a movie, taking a hike, having a picnic, going shopping, talking about your goals and dreams, taking dance lessons.
Supporting Fact 1C: Waiting to have sex until you are married builds self-discipline and ensures that you will not infect your life partner with a disease.	Supporting Fact 2C: If you do engage in sexual relations before marriage, you run a greater risk of becoming pregnant or causing a pregnancy, and/ or performing poorly in school–or dropping out of school due to infection or pregnancy.	Supporting Fact 3C: There are so many things to do that are fun without the pressure of sex and all that comes with it. You can talk about what you will be doing in 10 years, your dreams, goals and life aspirations.

TABLE 13.2: MESSAGE MAP ON UNDERAGE DRINKING AND DRIVING

BACKGROUND (THIS SECTION IS NOT INCLUDED IN A MESSAGE MAP. I HAVE INCLUDED IT TO HELP SET THE CONTEXT FOR THIS MAP): THIS CONVERSATION TOOK PLACE IN MY OFFICE BETWEEN A FATHER AND HIS SON. THE 17-YEAR-OLD SON HAD COME HOME FROM A PARTY WITH THE SMELL OF ALCOHOL ON HIS BREATH. THE FATHER CALLED ME AND WANTED ME TO TALK TO HIS SON ABOUT THE DANGERS OF DRINKING AND DRIVING. I ASKED THE FATHER TO COME IN FOR A SESSION BEFORE BRINGING HIS SON TO THE OFFICE. I ASSIGNED THE FATHER TO WORK WITH THE BOY'S MOTHER (PARENTS ARE DIVORCED) IN PREPARING A MESSAGE MAP. I EXPLAINED THAT THEY (THE MOM AND DAD) WOULD BE DOING MOST OF THE TALKING. I REVIEWED THE PROCESS OF DEVELOPING A MAP, AND THEY WENT AWAY WITH THE AGREEMENT THAT THEY WOULD WORK TOGETHER TO PREPARE MESSAGES IN ANTICIPATION TO THE FOLLOWING DIALOGUE AND QUESTION. THE MAP THEY BROUGHT TO THE OFFICE THE NEXT WEEK IS OUTLINED BELOW. THEY MET WITH ME FOR ABOUT 15 MINUTES BEFORE THEIR UNSUSPECTING SON CAME INTO THE ROOM. BY THE TIME THEIR SON ENTERED THE SESSION, HIS PARENTS WERE PREPARED AND DID A BRILLIANT JOB OF ARTICULATING THEIR ANSWERS TO HIS QUESTIONS.

Anticipated Question and Comments: I don't see what the big deal is with what I did. My parents are overreacting. I only had one beer before I drove home from the party. I was in total control. What's wrong with having one drink before driving?

Opening Statement: The father said: "Son, your mother and I love you and want what's best for you."

Message 1:	Message 2:	Message 3:
It's against the law.	It's dangerous.	It's harmful and addictive.

Supporting Fact 1A: We have no tolerance laws in our state.	Supporting Fact 2A: Each year 5,000 teens ages 16 to 20 die due to fatal injuries caused in a car crash (male deaths are 1.5 times higher than female deaths).	Supporting Fact 3A: The most serious effect of teenage drinking is that it leads to adult dependence. The National Institute on Alcohol Abuse and Alcoholism reports that teens who start drinking before the age of 15 are 4 times more likely to develop an alcohol addiction than those who do not begin drinking before the legal age of 21.
Supporting Fact 1B: If you had been pulled over, you would have gone to jail for at least one day.	Supporting Fact 2B: Thirty-one percent of drivers 15 to 20 who died in traffic accidents had been drinking.	Supporting Fact 3B: Alcohol may also serve as a "gateway drug" into more serious drug use.
Supporting Fact 1C: If your breath results were over .08, you would have been fined, your license would have been completely suspended for one year, and you would have been required to complete 40 hours of community service.	Supporting Fact 2C: Each year, 400,000 teens are seriously injured in car accidents.	Supporting Fact 3C: Alcohol poisoning can cause a person to go into a coma or it can cause death.

If time allows, present the key messages and supporting information contained in a message map using the *Triple T Model*: 1) Tell your child what you are going to tell them, i.e., key messages; 2) Tell them more, i.e., supporting information; (3) Tell them again what you told them, i.e., repeat key messages.

Again, it is important that you study and practice the use of message maps before delivering them to your children. This will allow you to take advantage of opportunities to re-emphasize or bridge to key messages when you are addressing a variety of questions in a difficult conversation.

When using your maps, do your best to stay on the prepared messages in the message map; avoid "winging it." By staying on task, you will see through the "smoke and mirrors" created by your child's resistance.

Perhaps most important in this process is to be honest. Always tell the truth. Nothing undermines your credibility faster than lying.

In conclusion, message maps are a viable tool for parents who place a high priority on effective communication related to serious issues that they will invariably face when raising teenagers. Using these maps better ensures that information discussed around difficult issues has the optimum chance of being heard, understood, and remembered.

CHAPTER 14

COUNSELING YOUR CHILDREN

P rivate, one-on-one communication is often called counseling. My experience has been that many think they do it well, without training. The fact is, most people can counsel, but it does require knowledge and skills to transform a one-way monologue into a two-way dialogue. In short, the "counselor" must learn to speak in a way that ensures the "counselee" will listen in ways that ensure he or she will talk.

As with communication, the ability to counsel your children is key to implementing and evaluating your parenting plan. Counseling can be quite effective if the proper principles are applied. These include 1) meeting one-on-one in a private setting, 2) letting your child do most of the talking, 3) listening to all your child has to say, 4) keeping what is said confidential, 5) striving to make your child understand that you are hearing everything he or she says by repeating back—in your own words—what you think he or she said, 6) being patient and remaining calm and collected regardless of what is said (If you get upset, communication will stop and you will have to work to regain the trust of your child), and 7) making appropriate suggestions in a sensitive way.

If you want to be an effective counselor to your children, you must be an effective listener. Why? Because if you do not carefully listen to what your child is saying, you will not gain a good understanding of the causes and severity of any given problem. Without this insight, it is nearly impossible to give good counsel.

I like to follow a six-step process when counseling my children. These steps are: 1) listening to understand the problem, how severe it is, and how long it has persisted; 2) paraphrasing what I have heard to reassure the child that I am listening and to determine whether I understand what they are saying; 3) asking what he or she thinks is causing the problem; 4) asking what he or she can do to overcome the problem; 5) asking what he or she thinks others can do to help; and 6) providing guidance that will allow him or her to make his or her own decisions in full view of the possible consequences (see the example in Table 7). I believe that if you love your children, you will not allow them to make self-destructive decisions without bringing the consequences of these decisions to their attention. In view of this, I often point out to our children that, although they are free to make decisions throughout their lives, they will typically have very little control over the consequences.

To reiterate what I have said about communication, one of the most important things you can do to set up opportunities for counseling is to get in the habit of meeting with your child on a regularly scheduled basis to discuss how things are going. These sessions should be held in a private setting and should provide an opportunity for your child to do most of the talking. Parents who insist on doing all the talking and demand that what their children say in return is consistent with what the parent wants to hear typically shut down communication all together. They simply teach their child how to say what they, the parents, want to hear instead of what the child is actually thinking or wants to say.

When you reflect on Figure 1 in the first chapter of the book, you will realize that this approach is a coping response by the parent and the child. The parent is coping to relieve the stress caused by what the child has said or done that is inconsistent with the parent's expectations. And the child is coping with the stress caused by the parent's interrogation. In both cases, these coping responses bring temporary relief. However, over the long term, because the parent is not willing to hear the truth and the child believes telling the truth is dangerous, things tend to get worse rather than better over time.

If you want to truly communicate with your child, you need to speak in a way that your child will listen and listen in a way that your child will speak. Any other approach may give temporary relief but inevitably causes a breakdown in communication.

To encourage my children to talk about a variety of things that I want to monitor during a counseling session, I have a list of items that I usually go over, such as school, teachers, friends, family, hobbies, favorite things to do, problems, and so on. I review these items in a regularly scheduled, private meeting with each child. If things are going well for a child, the private meetings can occur about one a month. When things are not going well, I meet with the struggling child on a more frequent basis.

With older teenagers, it is more difficult to schedule formal meetings. However, with some planning you can set the stage for a teachable counseling session. In my case, this type of session occurred during a one-on-one game of basketball, when riding horses in the woods, while walking on the beach, and while attending concerts together. The point is, whenever your children really like to talk, you should be prepared to listen and provide feedback.

APPLICATION OF THE SIX-STEP COUNSELING MODEL

1. Listening to understand the problem, how severe it is, and how long it has persisted. For example, Nick walks in after school and throws his books on the floor like he's upset. I let him settle down a bit and then say, "Hey Nick, do you have some time to talk?" (Nick) "Yes, I guess so." I find a private place and I ask him, "How are things?" (Nick) "Not good." (Me) "Go on." (Nick yells) "I hate life." I remain calm and say, "Go on." (Nick) "Nothing is going right for me." (Me) "Can you give me some examples of some of the things that you're having difficulty with?" (Nick) "I hate riding my bus." (Me) "What is it about riding the bus that upsets you." (Nick) "I just hate it, okay?!" (Me) "How long have you been having difficulties on the bus?" (Nick) "All week." (Me), "Do you hate riding both to and from school, or is it one or the other?" (Nick) "Both ways."

2. Paraphrasing what I have heard to reassure the child I am listening. "So all week you've been having trouble on the bus ride to and from school?" (Nick) "Yes, that's what I said, isn't it?" (Me) "Just wanted to make sure I understand you."

3. Asking what he or she thinks is causing the problem, and if he or she has no ideas, ask in a sensitive way if it could be something that has come to my mind. "So what is it that is causing the problem?" (Nick) "This new kid." (Me) "New kid?" (Nick) "A new kid started riding the bus this week, and he sits behind me and thumps me on the head." (Me) "Why does he do that?" (Nick) "He's a jerk! I can't stand him! Everybody thinks he's cool and whenever he thumps me, they all laugh!" (Me) "It sounds embarrassing." (Nick) "What do you think? Of course it is!" (Me) "Does he know it bothers you when he thumps you? That is, have you asked him to stop?" (Nick) "Not really." (Me) "Why is it that you haven't told him how you feel?" (Nick) "I don't want him to think I'm a wimp." (Me) "Do you thump him back?" (Nick) "No, but I feel like punching him in the face!" (Me) "What would happen if you punched him?" (Nick) "He's twice as big as I am. He'd kill me!"

4. Asking what he or she can do to overcome the problem and, if he or she can't think of anything, making appropriate suggestions as they come to mind. If a child does come up with ideas, I try to help him or her think about the consequences of acting on them. "What can you do to prevent the problem?" (Nick) Smack him in the face!" (Me) "Will that stop him from thumping you?" (Nick) "Probably not." (Me) "What else could you do?" (Nick) "Sit in the front of the bus." (Me) "How would that help?" (Nick) "He always sits in the back where I like to sit." (Me) "What else could you do?" (Nick) "Tell him to cut it out!" (Me) "Are there any other things you might try?" (Nick) "Not that I can think of."

5. Asking what he or she thinks others can do to help, and if he or she can't think of anything, I make appropriate suggestions. "Can anyone on the bus give you some help?" (Nick) "I could tell the bus driver, but then I would really be a nerd." (Me) "I could pick you up after school for a week to take the new kid's mind off thumping you." (Nick) "That may work, but not yet. I'm going to sit in front by my nerd friend, Lenny. Maybe the kid will leave me alone. If not, I'll get a ride from you."

6. Providing guidance that will allow him or her to make his or her own decisions in full view of the possible consequences. "Sounds like a plan, son. If sitting by Lenny doesn't work, I'll be happy to give you a ride for a while." (Nick) "I've gotta go meet some friends. See you later." (Me) "Be home for dinner or die a slow cruel death of starvation, little dude. And don't forget, little dude, I love you!" (Nick) "I won't be late. See you for dinner. I like you, too." (wink)

CHAPTER 15

MEDIATING CONFLICTS

J ust as mediation skills are required in a business setting to bring two parties together on a particular issue, mediation is also required in parenting. In fact, at times it seems like conflict mediation (diffusing arguments) is our most common parenting activity. This is particularly true when we are in close quarters, such as traveling in a car or sitting together in a family meeting.

The primary purpose of mediation is to help your children come to an amicable resolution when they are in conflict. The mediation strategy I recommend is described here in Table 15.1 .

TABLE 15.1: CONFLICT MEDIATION STRATEGY

- Meet separately with the children who are in conflict.
- Listen carefully to both sides of the argument.
- Solicit and discuss possible solutions to the conflict.
- Attempt to get both sides to agree to a solution. If not, decide on a solution and enlist the support of both sides.
- Specify consequences that will result if the conflict flares up again.
- Agree to meet again to discuss progress.
- Reward progress and/or apply consequences to non-compliant child.

SECTION II:

TEACHING TO ENSURE GOOD HEALTH AND GOOD CHARACTER

INTRODUCTION

S ection II focuses on one of the most important roles an effective parent can play in the lives of their children. The role I am referring to is that of a teacher. Professional teachers play a critical role in the lives of our youth. However, their academic training does not touch on many of the things that children must know to ensure their success in life. This is where a parent plays such a crucial training role.

To be effective in your role as a teacher, it is important to understand and apply correct principles in deciding what to teach and how to teach these things. To help you do these things effectively, I have provided you with the following: 1) a list of possible topics that you may want to cover, 2) a tool that can help you systematically decide which topics you will teach, 3) a description of a variety of teaching methods you can use, 4) information pertaining to developmental and psychological considerations in teaching, 5) guidance on how to develop a lesson plan around a particular topic, and 6) some sample lesson plans and lesson ideas that you can either teach or use as examples of how to prepare your own lesson plans. I have also provided a number of principles you should be familiar with when teaching.

CHAPTER 16

DECIDING WHAT TO TEACH

In the first section of the book, I explained the steps of creating a *Family Management Plan.* Just like with family management, the first step I recommend that you take in your efforts to teach your children to have good health and character is to systematically plan what you will teach by developing a *Family Teaching Plan* (FTP). Your FTP will function as the equivalent to a business training manual. While businesses formulate training plans that include all the training needs of their employees and the training activities they will employ to meet these needs, an FTP should include the things you want your children to know and do so they can be healthy, safe, and live up to their potential as individuals, members of your/their family, and members of society at-large.

I recommend a five-step process for developing an FTP. Step 1 requires listing those things you want your children to know, that is, what you want to teach them. To complete this step, you and your spouse should brainstorm all the basic life lessons you want your children to learn. Start with the big things, like "visualizing world peace," and move toward the smaller things, like "visualize looking both ways before crossing the street." Obviously, these things will vary depending on the age of your children. In any case, you should go through this process of deciding what to teach on a regularly scheduled basis to make sure you are teaching those things that are best suited to the needs and age of each child. To help you get started, I have provided you with an extensive list of topics you may want to cover. This list is displayed in Table 16.1.

While on a recent retreat to the mountains to celebrate our 25th wedding anniversary, my wife and I went through the process of deciding what we want to teach our 9-year-old and 16-year-old sons before they graduate from high school. Obviously, they are at very different stages, so we considered each boy separately. To organize our thinking about what we want them to know and do, we discussed their needs in terms of five dimensions important to their health and well-being: social, physical, intellectual, emotional, and spiritual. This organizing framework is based on my beliefs that 1) all people are multi-dimensional beings, 2) we all have needs in these areas, and 3) these needs must be satisfied to ensure that we have good health and well-being. (Please note that I have provided a sample lesson plan, *Acquiring The Dimensions of Health and Well-Being*, in the back of the book to illustrate how you can teach this idea to your children).

With these ideas in mind, we started with our 16-year-old. We asked ourselves, what are Joshua's social, physical, intellectual, emotional, and spiritual needs at this point in his life? That is, what does he need to know, feel, and do to be a balanced, healthy teenager and to eventually become a happy, healthy, productive adult? After discussing our teenager, we talked about Jordan's (our 9-year-old) needs. Once again, these discussions about needs are the first step required to complete the FTP.

Step 2 of the FTP calls for prioritizing this list of training needs and selecting those areas you will emphasize over a specific time period. Your effectiveness as a teacher will be greatly enhanced if you focus your efforts on one topic at a time. You cannot teach your children everything, so prioritize and focus your efforts on those things you deem to be most important and that are not likely to be taught by other institutions that your child is involved with, such as school or church.

Step 3 of the FTP step involves defining each of the things you plan to focus on. For example, if you plan to focus on the importance of regular exercise, clearly state what you want your child to know and do with regard to physical exercise, both as a child and as an adult. If you are trying to instill a work ethic, decide what you want your child to know and do in this area.

Step 4 is to develop a strategy to address each topic in your training efforts. Once again, if you plan to teach the importance of regular exercise, your strategy might be to take your children on a walk at a park at least four times per week. As your children grow older, you can explain the benefits of exercise, including: 1) improves concentration, 2) builds self-confidence, 3) increases creativity, 4) helps you relax, 5) reduces stress level, and 6) keeps weight within a desired range. When selecting a teaching strategy, remember that personal examples, for better or for worse, are powerful communicators. That is, a parent who does not exercise on a regular basis will no doubt have a more difficult time convincing a child of the importance and benefits of exercise than a parent who participates in regular physical activity (preferably with the child).

TABLE 16.1: LESSON IDEAS

Character	Family	Health	Safety	Social
work ethic	family support	addictions	firearms	dating
responsibility	parental	puberty/	water safety	positive
attitude	standards	sexuality	seatbelts	friends
honesty	respect for	alcohol and	home safety	pressure
perseverance	parents	other drugs	fire safety	interviewing
moderation	mate selection	tobacco	accident	for a job
self-control	marriage	grooming	prevention	etiquette
self-respect	parental roles	health care	violence	manners
respect for	birth	services	abuse	assertiveness
others	separation	personal	first aid skills	friendship
self-esteem	and divorce	hygiene	self-defense	skills
generosity	support	consumer	electric	respecting
	services	health	storms	authority
	love	food labels	floods	discrimination
	traditions	nutrition	tornadoes	citizenship
	genealogy/	physical		sportsmanship
	history	fitness		how to avoid
	abuse	stress		gangs
		emotions		

Life Skills	Education	Spirituality	Boundaries	Finances
critical thinking	studying for	prayer	parental	budgeting
communication	tests	religion	standards	checkbook
conflict	homework	faith	parental	saving
resolution	note-taking	voluntary	discipline	investing
mediation	time	service	personal	credit cards
decision-	management	golden rule	standards	charitable
making	reading	reverence	respecting	giving
planning	college	meditation	authority	fund raising
media literacy	selection	pornography		purchasing
motivation		death		negotiation

Both parents must participate honestly and openly (cooperate and work together) to ensure uniformity and consistency in the formulation and implementation of the plan. Children readily detect inconsistencies among parents and often exploit these divisions to their advantage.

If you are a single parent and rely heavily on another caregiver while working, you may want to involve this person in the planning process. At least inform this individual of what you are trying to accomplish in raising your children.

Whether you have a partner or are a single parent, it is important to acknowledge that others have an influence on your children during the course of their development. You may want to share your plan with close family members and friends who are exposed to your children on a regular basis. This will enable you to enlist their support in reinforcing those things you are trying to teach your children and will ensure that when they are around your children, they will try to do and say things that are in support of your own efforts.

As with developing a *Family Management Plan*, a side benefit that comes from working through the *Family Teaching Plan* steps with your spouse is found in the process required to arrive at a plan that you both agree on. This process requires good communication, self-disclosure, negotiation, and compromise. If this approach is taken seriously by investing the time and energy required to "get your act together," your teaching efforts will become more and more refined and effective over time. This refinement process will necessitate changes in the parenting plan as family circumstances change. Consider going on an annual retreat where you and your spouse can, without distractions, clarify and refine your plan. This retreat should be considered a time when the major strategies for parenting are "ironed out." The detail work on the plan should be an ongoing process whereby you meet together on a regularly scheduled basis (weekly or monthly) to discuss current issues and new ideas that may necessitate modifying the plan to meet the children's changing needs. Once again, these regularly scheduled meetings can help keep "help-mates" together on the particulars of their parenting strategy. For single parents, revisiting the plan on a regular basis can also be a time for reflection and refinement.

Once you have decided what principles you would like to teach your children, it is time to implement your plan of action. To find out whether or not you are having an impact, it is important that you assess how your children are progressing. Yogi Bera once said, "You can observe a lot just by watching."

You can observe your children at any time. When you create an environment wherein children feel comfortable "being themselves," then you will have ample opportunity to discover how they are doing. In fact, parents who stay close to their children often get updates directly from their children. These updates can come in the form of oral reports or, as is often the case when children get older, body language. Once again, however, parents must stay close to their children so they can pick up the subtle nuances in their behavior and so the child feels comfortable in sharing his or her feelings. One thing is certain: When parents use harsh discipline and chronic criticism when things are not just right, the child learns not to communicate unless things are going well. And in turn, the parents are often uninformed until it is too late to help a child through a difficult spot, and then serious remedial action is required. For obvious reasons, this is especially poignant when a child commits suicide.

Step 5 on the FTP is designed to help with the process of following up on your children's progress. It requires transferring what you plan to focus on during a specified time period onto the

Progress Tracker displayed in Table 16.2.

TABLE 16.2: PROGRESS TRACKER			
Knowledge Questions [1]	Need? [2]	Behavior Questions [3]	Need? [4]
Respect			
Honesty			
Responsibility			
Self-control			
Work			
Service			
Success			
Exercise			
Diet			

1. Things you want your child to know.
2. Discrepancy between what child knows and what he or she should know. Once you have identified a need, it is useful to find out why the need exists (i.e., the cause). If you know the cause(s) or why the child does not know or do what he or she should, then you can more readily come up with a solution(s) that addresses what is contributing to the need.
3. Things you would like the child to do.
4. Discrepancy between what the child does and what you would like the child to do.

Note: Many would argue that it is not the parent's role to try to shape the behaviors of their children, and that the role of a parent begins and ends with transmitting information. This is a nice idea, but it is not practical. When a child acts out or is not fulfilling designated assignments, a benevolent parent will provide appropriate consequences that are designed to shape the child's behavior in the best interest of the child. For example, if a small child screams incessantly, it may be appropriate to place the child in time-out. Or if a teenager is caught and arrested for DWI, it may be in the young person's best interest to withhold the car keys.

As you will see, the *Progress Tracker* has four columns. Column 1 provides a space for you to list those things you want your children to know. Column 2 is for checking off when your children do not know something you want them to know. Column 3 provides space to list things you want your children to do. Lastly, in column 4 you designate a deficiency in a desired behavior. The form should only include those things you will focus on during a given period of time.

Remember, you cannot teach your children everything at once. Therefore, focus on those things that are most relevant to their personal needs, ages, and circumstances.

Because there is so much to teach, parents often do not know where to begin. A good starting point is to focus on meeting the informational and behavioral needs of your children. As you identify and note discrepancies between what behaviors you want to see in your children (as specified on the *Progress Tracker*) and what you actually observe, you have identified a need (the check marks you place in columns 2 or 4). Focus your efforts on meeting these needs. As one individual put it, "When we deal with generalities we rarely succeed; when we deal in specifics we rarely fail."

The process just described may seem time-consuming and burdensome. It is both. The alternative, however, is parenting without clear direction. The consequence of not taking the time and making the effort to "decide" where you are going is illustrated in the following Aesop's fable, *The Man, the Boy and the Donkey* (Æsop. (Sixth century B.C.) Fables. The Harvard Classics. 1909–14):

A MAN and his son were once going with their Donkey to market. As they were walking along by its side a countryman passed them and said: "You fools, what is a Donkey for but to ride upon?"

So the Man put the Boy on the Donkey and they went on their way. But soon they passed a group of men, one of whom said: "See that lazy youngster, he lets his father walk while he rides."

So the Man ordered his Boy to get off, and got on himself. But they hadn't gone far when they passed two women, one of whom said to the other: "Shame on that lazy lout to let his poor little son trudge along."

Well, the Man didn't know what to do, but at last he took his Boy up before him on the Donkey. By this time they had come to the town, and the passers-by began to jeer and point at them. The Man stopped and asked what they were scoffing at. The men said: "Aren't you ashamed of yourself for overloading that poor Donkey of yours—you and your hulking son?"

The Man and Boy got off and tried to think what to do. They thought and they thought, till at last they cut down a pole, tied the Donkey's feet to it, and raised the pole and the Donkey to their shoulders. They went along amid the laughter of all who met them till they came to Market Bridge, when the Donkey, getting one of his feet loose, kicked out and caused the Boy to drop his end of the pole. In the struggle the Donkey fell over the bridge, and his fore-feet being tied together he was drowned.

"That will teach you," said an old man who had followed them: "You will not succeed if you have no plan."

The worst-case scenarios of parenting without forethought or direction can be devastating. The examples of the problems that occur in homes where youth are not given clear direction are endless. Planning takes time and is worth every minute invested.

CHAPTER 17

TEACHING METHODS

In most cases, the way you teach—your teaching method—is as important as what you teach. This chapter presents a number of different teaching methods and a description of each method. Teaching methods are those learning activities used to communicate what you want your children to know and do about a particular subject or behavior. When planning a lesson, you will select one or more of these methods to accomplish the purposes of your lesson. The methods I describe here include 1) discussion, 2) question and answer, 3) computerized learning, 4) storytelling, 5) media-oriented, 6) visualization, 7) discovery or problem-solving, 8) lecture, 9) directed independent learning, 10) family outing, 11) demonstration, 12) role-playing and dramatization, 13) modeling, and 14) mixed methods.

Discussion Method: This method is effective for developing respect for the ideas and opinions of others. When applying this method, you should do a considerable amount of planning to ensure that the discussion does not get out of control. You should also designate a moderator. You can use this method when leading a discussion about what is the best way to overcome a particular problem the family is experiencing.

For example, if the children are not performing their assigned chores as they should, you could hold a council to review what tasks need to be done to maintain the house. You could allow the children to express their opinions about the best ways to get all of these things done. Because this method allows everyone to contribute ideas, there is often more "buy-in." If the children's ideas are adopted, they are more likely to help implement their ideas.

Question and Answer Method: This method is much like the discussion method and can either be child- or parent-centered. If it is child-centered, the parents encourage the child to ask questions about a particular topic to gain more information. For example, the child could be encouraged to ask you about your childhood, such as what was hard about growing up, what was fun, what were some of the good things that happened to you, or how you overcame your problems.

If this method is parent-centered, the parents can ask questions to generate a discussion on a particular topic. For example, you can ask children a series of questions about their favorite foods, their favorite activities, their favorite people, problems that give them the most difficulty, problems that kids their age are facing, their most important goals, their most significant fears, and so on.

Whether child- or parent-centered, when first applying this method it is best to give everyone advance notice so all family members have time to prepare questions and think about the issue. The back-and-forth that occurs using this method is especially helpful in teaching good two-way communication skills. It is also a good method for obtaining both positive and negative feedback that can help create mutual understanding.

This method is an ideal way for you, as a parent, to informally transmit your personal values. The answers you give in response to your children's questions will be couched in your personal belief system, which will, in most cases, become your children's belief system until they are old enough to establish their own. Through this method, you can model appropriate ways of asking and answering questions.

Ask questions that stimulate thinking and encourage your children to respond. Questions can be asked that direct your children to search for information, think about what they have found, and apply the information to their personal lives.

Computerized Learning Method: There are a number of computer programs on the market that are designed to teach children a variety of lessons: math, reading comprehension, spelling, typing, anatomy and physiology, foreign languages, and so on. If you purchase and become familiar with these games, they can be used to help augment your child's learning at school and foster interaction between you and your child at home.

In addition, there are a number of reference programs that you can suggest to your child when you want him or her to develop independent learning skills. I often tell my children when they are seeking information that they can find answers to most of their questions on the World Wide Web. Simply assign your child to research a particular topic and then report back to the family on what he or she finds. This is with the understanding that children's activity on the web should be monitored and they should be taught about Internet safety (such as not giving out personal information).

Storytelling Method: This technique can be used to teach lessons in an entertaining manner. As long as the story is relevant to the child and captures the child's interest, it is likely that he or she will listen and learn from the story. This is particularly true if you prepare your children to listen for certain points that you want them to gain from the story and then talk about these points afterwards.

Media-Oriented Method: Using media to convey information can add variety to your lesson and stimulate learning. Slides, photographs, music, video, overhead slides, and pictures can all be used to present a main message or to enhance messages conveyed by other methods. We have several flip charts with many different pictures that we have used to teach a variety of lessons. You can use pictures of firemen, policemen, doctors, teachers, and insurance salespeople when talking about different vocational options. We have numerous videos that we use to reinforce lessons about manners, being concerned about the welfare of others, and so on. We have also purchased a number of video and CDs that tell stories about famous individuals throughout history who displayed character traits we want our children to incorporate into their own lives.

Visualization Method: This method requires those who use it to close their eyes and imagine something. This technique is often used when teaching people to relax. It can also be used to help people change the way they think about the things they experience. For example, if a person or a situation in your daily life causes stress-inducing thoughts, you can attempt to change the way you think of the situation or person (*cognitive restructuring*) by visualizing something positive about the situation—or by visualizing another situation or person altogether. You can even start singing a song or repeating a favorite quote to help you calm down. We know a person who begins silently reciting a verse in the Bible when he gets anxious (Proverbs chapter 3, verse 5).

Discovery or Problem-Solving Method: This approach to

teaching is effective with all ages. It entails setting up a problem that your children are asked to solve. For example, present your teenager with a problem that many families commonly deal with, such as finances. Each child could be given a set amount of play money and told to practice budgeting their expenses for one month. Then provide your children with a variety of things that they can choose to spend their money on: fun things, or things like bills and car payments. Once they have "spent" their money, if they chose to purchase non-necessities before or instead of paying bills, you can point out the consequences of their decisions (such as no lights, telephone, food, or air-conditioning, depending on what they neglected to pay). This type of problem-solving activity can help you children understand why they must be careful about how much they spend and on what.

Lecture Method: This method usually involves standing or sitting in front of your children and imparting specific information. For example, you may have decided that you want your children to do certain chores, so you review the chore list to make each child aware of his or her assignments. Or you may explain a certain safety hazard and what each person should do to avoid the hazard.

The advantage of this method is that a great deal of information can be imparted. The disadvantage is that it is difficult to hold your children's attention if you use this method too liberally, particularly with young children, who have very short attention spans. In fact, lecturing should rarely be used with pre-teens. Even teenagers, who tend to be accustomed to the highly stimulating images and messages presented through the media and popular music, often become bored when information is presented in a lecture format. Hence, the lecture method should be used sparingly and/or briefly.

Directed Independent Learning Method: This is an important method for teaching children to take the initiative and the responsi-bility to learn on their own. For example, you can assign a child to find a book on a particular topic, read the book, and report back to the family on what he or she has learned. Another example is to encourage children to read the newspaper and report back on a news event that captured their interest. You can then ask your children to find other sources on the same topic and make additional reports as more information about the event becomes available. This approach teaches young people how to probe deeper into the events that interest them. Initially, you should both structure and provide direction in this process until your children understand how to proceed on their own. For example, when you assign a particular topic you can also provide ideas about where to get information, how to summarize it, and how to present it in a concise and interesting manner.

Family Outing Method: Taking your children to a museum, farm, zoo, factory, hospital, court, or state park is a method of teaching that, in a school setting, is often referred to as a field trip. Family outings can help broaden your child's contacts in your community and provide them with a broader base of experience upon which to make decisions and interpret the world around them. For example, if you take your teenager to visit children in a pediatric oncology ward at a local hospital, your teen will gain a greater appreciation of health and the difficulties others must learn to cope with. This type of experience can help reinforce knowledge of compassion, courage, disease, health services, and so on. These outings should be well-planned so children are prepared for the experience and are looking for certain things that you want them to learn about.

Demonstration Method: Demonstration is a highly effective method, particularly if you are good at what you demonstrate. In fact, studies have shown that children often learn better from demonstrations than they do from verbal communication, especially when learning a skill. For example, if you want your child to clean a bathroom or mow the lawn, it is much better to work with him or her a few times and show what you expect than to simply say, "mow the lawn." Do not expect children to automatically absorb things that you often take for granted. Do not be a "gotcha" parent who tells kids to do something and then gets upset when they do not do it exactly like you told them to. It is hard to visualize complex behavior. In short, demonstrate what you want done as often as possible.

Role-playing and Dramatization Method: Children of all ages love dramatization and role-playing. This method involves writing or informally explaining a script that you ask your children to act out. You can also ask them to ad-lib a situation using their own creativity and imagination. For example, if you want to teach your children the skills required to resist peer pressure to smoke or drink, you can have them take turns tempting and resisting temptation.

This method goes along with demonstration. Once you demonstrate a behavior or skill, you can ask your children to role-play the skill to determine whether or not they have mastered the technique. You can, for example, demonstrate how you want your children to talk to one another—in soft, respectful tones—and then have them role-play what you have demonstrated.

Modeling Method: Perhaps the most effective technique of all, in terms of transmitting ideas about living, is role-modeling. For the most part, what your kids observe in your attitudes and actions is what you will eventually observe in their own attitudes and behaviors. They have the unique ability to see past your words. Modeling serves to teach and reinforce the messages you want to teach. This is why it is so important that you strive to become the person you want each of your children to become.

Mixed Methods: I like to use a variety of methods whenever I teach lessons. Just as a good cook uses a variety of main and side dishes to prepare a good meal, my wife and I have found that using a variety of methods ensures a much better lesson. Never "serve too much" of the same thing, or your children will tire of it and their learning will be inhibited. A very simple example of how we have used multiple methods is when we attempted to teach good table manners. We first explained the importance of using good table manners. We then demonstrated what we meant by displaying these same manners. Finally, we played a video that showed young people having dinner and modeling both good and bad manners.

We have incorporated a variety of methods in the sample lesson plans provided at the end of this section. You should also try using a variety of methods when you prepare your own plans. As you become more experienced with the various methods, you will discover what we have: Some methods will work better with your family than others, and different methods are more effective with different age groups. When our children were very young, we told stories, sang songs, and played games. Now that we have older children, we have more guided discussions that are prompted by issues we think are relevant to the needs of each child.

CHAPTER 18
DEVELOPMENTAL CONSIDERATIONS IN TEACHING

The lessons you prepare should be conducive to the age (developmental levels) and interest levels of the children. Although there are no set rules about what should be taught at the various developmental levels, there is agreement among most psychologists that children develop logical thinking in a more or less orderly sequence. This means that before a child can master a higher-level concept, he or she must master a lower one. When teaching very young children, the concepts you teach should be very basic. These basic ideas provide a necessary foundation for the more advanced concepts that will follow. That is, build the foundation of your child's "house of knowledge" before you put on the roof. Furthermore, when preparing lessons for young children, you should realize that they have short attention spans, they enjoy hands-on activities (play) more than talking, and they need very clear instructions. Therefore, lessons presented to youngsters should be brief and to the point and should involve some hands-on learning opportunities, even games that are adapted to the age of each child.

Perhaps the most important consideration here is personal relevance. Children of all ages are typically turned off by information that does not relate to them personally. Hence, when preparing a lesson, do what you can to present the main ideas in a context that is relevant to the age and developmental stage of the children. If you are planning to teach your teenage children about the negative effects of smoking cigarettes, rather than focusing on long-term consequences, such as lung cancer and emphysema, talk about the short-term negative effects of smoking, such as bad breath and social disapproval. A recent public service announcement used this approach with kids by relating such messages as, "When you kiss a smoker, it is like kissing an ashtray." Obviously, this message appeals to the immediate needs of teenagers, such as getting a date and being socially acceptable to their peers. A poster designed to prevent smoking among teenagers showed a box of rat poison alongside a cigarette and asked, "Did you know the same thing that is in rat poisoning is in cigarettes?" Once again, the message is simple but clear and relevant and uses a dramatic parallel to make a point, creating a higher-level cognitive message that teenagers can appreciate .

CHAPTER 19

PSYCHOLOGICAL CONSIDERATIONS IN TEACHING

U nderstanding and applying some basic psychological principles when you are preparing a lesson can increase the likelihood that your children will adopt the attitudes and actions that you believe are in their best interest. To this end, I endorse eight psychological conditions that leading social psychologists agree should exist if one expects an individual to adopt recommended attitudes or actions. In the context of parenting, this means that if you can create certain conditions around behaviors that you want your children to adopt, then it will be much more likely for them to adopt these behaviors. There actually is a science to parenting that can be applied to ensure better results. The eight conditions that, according to Dr. Marty Fishbein and his colleagues (1991), you should strive to create are displayed in Table 19.1.

TABLE 19.1: PSYCHOLOGICAL CONDITIONS IMPORTANT TO BEHAVIORAL COMPLIANCE

To increase the likelihood that your child will adopt or abstain from a certain behavior (homework, regular exercise, not using drugs, or delaying sex until marriage) he or she—

1. MUST form a strong positive intention (or make a commitment) to do what you recommend.

2. MUST have the skill(s) necessary to do what you recommend.

3. MUST have few environmental constraints that prevent him or her from doing what you recommend.

4. SHOULD believe that the advantages of doing what you recommend outweigh the disadvantages.

5. SHOULD perceive that there is more social pressure to do what you recommend than not to do it.

6. SHOULD believe what you recommend is consistent with his or her self-image and does not violate his or her personal standards.

7. SHOULD have a positive reinforcement for doing what you recommend he or she do.

8. SHOULD believe (have confidence) he or she can do what you recommend.

The first three conditions shown in Table 19.1 (i.e., intention, ability, and environmental constraints) are considered "necessary and sufficient" for inducing your child to behave in a certain way. In other words, for a given behavior to occur, your child must 1) have a strong positive commitment or intention to perform the behavior, 2) have the skills required to implement the behavior, and 3) live in an environment that is conducive to the behavior's occurrence. For example, if he or she is committed to delay sex until marriage; has the skills required to resist peer pressure to engage in sex; and has a supportive home, school, peer, and/or church environment, it is very likely that he or she will delay the onset of sexual activity.

The remaining five conditions (see the SHOULDS in Table 19.1) "are viewed as influencing the strength or intensity and direction of [your child's] intention to do what you want them to do ." In keeping with the example of delaying sexual activity, your child will be more likely to form a strong intention to delay sex if (4) he or she believes that this behavioral choice will result in more positive (e.g., freedom from guilt, better health) than negative (e.g., unwanted pregnancy or disease) outcomes; (5) he or she perceives more social pressure to delay sex than to engage in it; (6) he or she perceives that delaying the onset of sexual activity is consistent with his or her self-image and does not violate his or her personal or family standards; (7) his or her emotional reaction to delaying sex is positively reinforced; and 8) he or she is confident that he or she can delay sexual activity.

These same eight conditions apply to many (if not all) behaviors you want your children to adopt. For example, if you are striving to get your child to study on a regular basis, you should work to ensure that your child 1) makes a strong positive commitment to study every night, 2) has adequate study skills, 3) has a designated area to study without interruptions, 4) believes the choice to study will result in more positive (e.g., good grades, parental approval, less stress, success in life) than negative (e.g., placed on restriction by parents, no driver's license, not admitted to a preferred college) outcomes, 5) perceives more social pressure to study than to not study, 6) perceives that studying is consistent with his or her self-image and does not violate his or her personal standards, (7) has an emotional reaction to studying that has been positively reinforced, and 8) has confidence that he or she can indeed study. To further help you apply these principles, I have incorporated them into the sample lessons at the end of the book.

CHAPTER 20

CREATING AN ENVIRONMENT FOR LEARNING

Although it is not good to be overly rigid about the environment, it is necessary to establish and maintain an appropriate setting for learning. This can be accomplished by creating a congenial and informal atmosphere in which communication can flow openly. When possible, eliminate distractions such as the telephone or television.

Set standards for appropriate conduct during your family meetings and sensitively encourage everyone to adhere to these standards. As children get older, ask them for input as to what ground rules should apply to ensure order during family meetings. Remember, however, that the reason for bringing your family together is more about learning to talk and enjoy being together as a family than about starting and finishing a lesson. If you are not flexible and loving in your approach to these meetings, your children will dread them instead of look forward to them.

If you can see that a meeting is not going as planned because someone is irritable or has a need that is different from what you originally planned, do not hesitate to modify, delete, add insights or materials, or change course altogether to meet the needs of those you are teaching. I have been prepared to teach what I thought was an important lesson only to find that our children were exhausted and could not devote the necessary attention to learn the concept. With experience, I have learned to always have a back-up plan for times like these. I have made the decision to rent a video, go out for ice cream, play a game, or just talk. However, I always try to do something to preserve the habit of meeting together on a set night. If you do not do this, you run the risk of losing the habit.

CHAPTER 21

PREPARING A LESSON PLAN

To help you prepare to teach, I have provided you with guidance on how to develop a lesson plan, as shown in Table 12. In addition, I have provided you with 25 sample lesson plans that relate to one or more of the topic areas I have just described. Many of the sample lessons are quite extensive, so you may spend more than one session on each lesson.

If the topic is especially important for your family, you may even want to spend an entire month focusing on that topic. For example, the first lesson I suggest that you teach is the lesson on creating and maintaining a functional family. This lesson provides a foundation for what you are trying to accomplish with your family. Because the lesson is quite extensive, it should be subdivided, according to your needs, into many different, yet related lessons.

For example, the first lesson you teach on this topic could discuss the differences between functional and dysfunctional families. Subsequent lessons could then focus on the characteristics of a functional family by covering a single characteristic each week. In most cases, these characteristics include those things you uphold in your *Family Mission Statement*.

Another lesson that is likely to take up more than one session is resisting peer pressure. As is noted in our sample lesson plan on this topic, you could easily extend this lesson by incorporating a directed independent learning experience that could last for two or more weeks.

To reiterate, please do not feel like once you start discussing a particular lesson, you must finish it in one session or you must continue on with the lesson if your children want to talk about something else. If you doggedly stick to a lesson, your family sessions may begin to feel a lot like "school." Even though these family meetings provide the most important schooling your children will ever receive, the environment should be somewhat relaxed to ensure success.

The main point of your teaching activity is to set aside time to discuss issues that are important to you and your children. It is a time that everyone should enjoy—a time when everyone gets to participate freely.

You should also be aware that if you tend to dominate the discussions and/or always choose the lessons, your children may feel inhibited to talk. They will simply "shut down" in spite of their natural tendency to want to talk about or even challenge your ideas. I have learned that a child "convinced against his will is of the same opinion still (Dale Carnegie, How to Win Friends and Influence People.)

We have agreed that when we sit down and talk as a family on a weekly basis (even though we often veer away from what we plan to discuss), we achieve some measure of success. In fact, sometimes instead of having a lesson we play a game, eat a snack, and just talk. Sometimes we do not even finish the game. This is to say that children tend to be more engaged when they know their needs and preferences are more important than a lesson schedule.

TABLE 21.1: HOW TO DEVELOP A LESSON PLAN

TOPIC OF THE LESSON:

WHAT I WANT THEM TO KNOW
Record the knowledge objectives of the lesson plan. These statements should be brief and to the point. For example, if you want your child to know what the family rules are, state, "By the end of this lesson, my child will know what the family rules are." These statements will be used in connection with Progress Tracker.

WHAT I WANT THEM TO DO
Record the behavioral objectives of the lesson. That is, what you want your child to do as a result of this lesson. For example, "As a result of this lesson, my child will be able to properly vacuum the carpet in the living room," or "My child will be able to take a phone message relaying who called, why they called, whether or not they want their call returned and, if so, when to call back and at what number the caller can be reached."

WHAT I PLAN TO TEACH (What it is, why it's important, what they should know about it)
Record all the points you want to make during the lesson. This information should correspond with what is stated in your knowledge and behavioral objectives. For instance, if your knowledge objective is "to know what the family curfew is on Friday nights" and the behavioral objective is "to come in from a date before curfew" then, in this section, you will need to be explicit about what the curfew is and provide some incentive for compliance.

HOW I PLAN TO TEACH IT (My Methods)
Record the teaching methods that you will use to teach the things you have specified in the previous section. These include a variety of methods: lecture, media-oriented, discussion, question and answer, demonstration, and the like. I strongly recommend that you use a variety of methods whenever possible.

HOW I PLAN TO FIND OUT IF THEY KNOW AND DO WHAT I WANT THEM TO
Record your plan for following up to determine whether or not your lesson was effective. The Progress Tracker should be used for this purpose, in addition to observation and other appropriate means of determining whether or not your children/teenagers are on track.

HOW I PLAN TO REINFORCE WHAT I HAVE TAUGHT
Record your plans for reinforcing messages. Given that your children will likely be exposed to many messages that are contrary to what you teach them, reinforcing your message is crucial if you hope to have a lasting impact. Message reinforcement is like giving booster shots to ensure full immunity against diseases.

CHAPTER 22

SAMPLE LESSON PLANS

A s stated previously, I have provided you with a number of lesson plans. Some of these plans, however, are quite extensive and, in most instances, will take two or more sessions to teach. My hope is that after you have taught some of these plans, you will be able to use the guidance provided in Table 21.1 ("How to Develop a Lesson Plan") to develop your own plans.

As you will see, the first sample lesson I provide is entitled, "We Want to Have an Ideal Family." I have included this topic first because if you "start with the end in mind," it should be obvious that the goal of parenting is to have a maximally functional family.

WE WANT TO HAVE AN IDEAL FAMILY

WHAT I WANT THEM TO KNOW
- There are differences between functional and dysfunctional families.
- We, as your parents, want to have a highly functional family. There are things each of you can do to help us attain this goal.
- To have a functional family requires work on the part of every family member.

WHAT I WANT THEM TO DO
- Learn what it takes to have a functional family
- Do their part to help our family be functional

WHAT I PLAN TO TEACH
- We should be able to identify and to adopt positive characteristics of an ideal family (refer to our *Family Mission Statement*).
- Each family member can do to better to ensure that we have a functional family.

HOW I PLAN TO TEACH IT (MY METHODS)
- Ask family members to brainstorm the characteristics of a functional family.
- Ask them to brainstorm the characteristics of a dysfunctional family.
- Assign children to discuss a different characteristic of a functional family each week.
- Discuss a different functional characteristic every week, emphasizing what each person should do to incorporate these characteristics into his or her own life.

- Commit each child to work on one functional characteristic every week.
- Once all characteristics in our *Family Mission Statement* have been covered, commit children to continue working on improving themselves.
- Post a sign every week that displays the characteristic that the family has been challenged to work on for the week.
- After covering every functional characteristic, make a permanent display that lists those traits we want our family to continue to work on (i.e., our *Family Mission Statement*).

HOW I PLAN TO FIND OUT IF THEY KNOW AND DO WHAT I WANT THEM TO

- Observe how well they adhere to the functional family character traits.
- Hold one-on-One interviews using the *Progress Tracker* to determine if children can recognize, and are adopting, these character traits.

HOW I PLAN TO REINFORCE WHAT I HAVE TAUGHT

- I will set a good example by living these traits.
- I will post functional family traits and refer to them often.
- When I observe children deviating from desired traits, I will remind them that their actions are working against our goal to have a functional family.

WE BELIEVE IN BEING HONEST

WHAT I WANT THEM TO KNOW
- You should be honest in all your dealings.
- Even though it can be hard at times, honesty has many benefits.
- Half-truths are lies.
- Lies have many negative consequences.
- When you betray a confidence, you are being dishonest.
- When you slack off at work, you are being dishonest.

WHAT I WANT THEM TO DO
- Always tell the truth, regardless of the consequences
- Always be fair and honest in all their dealings with other people

WHAT I PLAN TO TEACH
- A person who is honest always tells the truth, does not tell half-truths or withhold important information when giving an account of a situation, and strives to treat everyone fairly.
- Honesty is the basis of any good relationship. If people are honest, you can trust them. People respect honesty. They are suspicious of those who are not honest.
- Our family believes you should be honest in all your dealings—both in the big things and the little things. Even though it can be hard at times, honesty has many benefits. If you are honest with us, your parents, we will reward you with more freedom because we know you can handle it and you will tell us the truth if there is a problem.
- Lying has many negative consequences. Liars are dishonest. They cannot be trusted because when it is in their best interest they will lie, distort the truth by telling half-truths, and so on. Those who lie get caught and suffer negative consequences.

- When someone tells you a secret, you should keep it confidential. People who betray confidences are dishonest and lose the trust of others.

HOW I PLAN TO TEACH IT (MY METHODS)
- Ask how people feel about those who are honest.
- Ask how people feel about those who lie.
- Brainstorm ways that people can be dishonest (little and big ways).
- Discuss negative things that can result when a person is dishonest.
- Tell a story illustrating consequences of lying: "The Boy Who Cried Wolf."
- Show a video that illustrates consequences of dishonesty and deception.

HOW I PLAN TO FIND OUT IF THEY KNOW AND DO WHAT I WANT THEM TO
- Observe the honesty of each child.
- Hold one-on-one interviews using *Progress Tracker* to determine what children know about honesty and how honest they are.

HOW I PLAN TO REINFORCE WHAT I HAVE TAUGHT
- Set a good example of honesty.
- Post a sign that says, "Honesty is Always the Best Policy."
- Read quotes every day that demonstrate that honesty is a good thing.

Parents, it should be understood that very young children (aged 7 and younger) often say things that are not true because they have vivid imaginations and desire adventure and fun. They often mistake their imagination for what is real. In such cases, you should help them sort out what is true and what is not. Because young children are not fully capable of knowing the difference between right and wrong, they should not be punished for such statements. If you do punish them at this stage of their development for something as simple as making up a "tall tale," you will be curtailing their imagination and inhibiting their natural desire to communicate all the wonderful things they feel and think as they experience the world for the first time.

WE BELIEVE IN MAKING AND SAVING MONEY

WHAT I WANT THEM TO KNOW
- There are many ways to make money. The best way is to work for it.
- You should manage your money with a budget.
- You should try to avoid debt.
- You should give 10 percent of your money to a charitable cause.
- You should always save 10 percent of what you make.
- We cannot give you money every time you ask for it, or buy you something every time you want it.

WHAT I WANT THEM TO DO
- Acquire knowledge and develop skills that they can use to make money
- Create a budget and manage their money accordingly
- Pay 10 percent of their earnings to our church
- Save 10 percent of their earnings

WHAT I PLAN TO TEACH
- There are many ways to make money. The best way is to work for it. You can do certain chores around the house that we will pay you for; you can mow lawns and do other odd jobs for our neighbors; and when you are old enough, you can get a job.
- Whenever you get paid, you should first give 10 percent to our church and then put 10 percent in a savings account or in your piggy bank. There are many people who, through no fault of their own, do not have enough food or money to cover their basic needs. Therefore, it is important to provide for the needs of those who are less fortunate than you. You can do this by donating a percentage of your earnings to your church. (In this regard, we have taught our

children that when a person is generous, God promises that his or her financial needs will always be met and that the money will go further. Once again, modify this principle in accordance with your family values.)

- You should manage the rest of your money with a budget.
- You prepare a budget by listing all the things you want to buy or activities you want to participate in during a specified period of time (a week or a month) on the left side of a piece of paper. On the right side of the paper, list the costs of these items. Total the column on the right. Remember, if the total is more than you earn, you will need to sacrifice an item in the left column, reduce the amount you spend on it, or increase your income. Making and following a budget like this will help you prioritize your expenditures. If you live within your budget, you will never go into debt. When you are young, we will help you buy things. As you get older, you will need to buy things for yourself. When you get to that point, you will be your "own person." It is a great feeling to be able to take care of your own needs. In sum, the purpose of a budget is to wisely control your money.
- The reason we cannot give you money every time you ask for it, or buy you something every time you want it, is because we have a limited income and if we spend more than we make, we will go into debt.
- Debt is incurred when you borrow money to buy things you cannot afford. It is a bad thing in most cases because you must work for money that is already spent. It can be very discouraging to make money and give it to someone else without receiving anything in return. Debt can cause you a lot of stress. Avoid debt as much as possible.

HOW I PLAN TO TEACH MY IDEAS (MY METHODS)
- Ask for ideas about how to make money.
- Review our family standards for charitable giving and saving money. (Make the points listed above.)
- Explain the importance of a budget.
- Show them the family budget and explain how it works.
- Help each child develop his or her own budget.
- Explain the importance of staying out of debt. Demonstrate how debt works.

- Watch a video on how to save money.
- Read a short book on how to save money.

HOW I PLAN TO FIND OUT IF THEY KNOW AND DO WHAT I WANT THEM TO
- Hold one-on-one Interviews using the *Progress Tracker* to determine what the children know about making and saving money, charitable giving, and debt, and ask them whether or not they are doing what we have suggested they do regarding these matters. For example:
  - Do you have a budget?
  - Are you referring to your budget every time you get paid?

HOW I PLAN TO REINFORCE WHAT I HAVE TAUGHT
- Help each child open a savings account.
- Help them make deposits in their savings and give money to their religious leaders or a charitable organization through the appropriate channels.
- Review the family budget at family council.
- Show them how we save money for a family vacation. When on vacation, remind children that the vacation was made possible only because of planning and saving.

WE BELIEVE IN WATCHING OUR WORDS

WHAT I WANT THEM TO KNOW

- Words are vehicles that carry messages that can do good or harm.
- It is important to use language to help rather than to hurt people.
- You can learn to use words that will help you make and keep friends.
- Profanity and vulgarity are unacceptable. Do not use them at any time.
- What you say reflects on you and our family, for good or bad.
- You should use courteous words that convey respect when talking to adults.

WHAT I WANT THEM TO DO

- Monitor the words they use and how they use them
- Use words and phrases in a way that builds people up rather than tears them down
- Abstain from gossip ("he said, she said")

WHAT I PLAN TO TEACH

- Words are vehicles that convey messages. Some words convey very good messages, and some convey very bad messages that can make people angry.
- Using profanity and vulgarity are in violation of our family rules. Profanity is language that shows disrespect for religious things, like saying the name of deity when you are upset. Many people are offended when these words are used.
- Vulgar words are crude or obscene words (cuss words) about body parts, body functions, or sex acts/organs that are characterized by lack of refinement, restraint, sensitivity, and good taste. Vulgar words convey ugly and aggressive messages and show disrespect for civil behavior. As with profanity, many people are offended by

vulgarity, for they believe that the use of these words in public is a violation of their privacy. As one person put it, "The use of profanity or vulgarity represents a feeble mind trying to express itself forcefully (Mark Twain)."

- Many people who use profanity and vulgarity claim the right to do so under freedom of speech. However, when they use these terms in public, they diminish the freedom of those who are offended by them. Such words are like second-hand smoke; those who object to profanity but who are in the same room as people who use profane and vulgar language must hear this language when it is spoken.
- Profanity and vulgarity are unacceptable. Do not use them at any time.
- What you say reflects on you and our family. If what you say is good, it can reflect positively. If it is crude, vulgar, and profane, it will most definitely reflect negatively.
- Using the right kinds of words can protect you and others from violence. If you use words that make people upset, it is possible that the offended person will use words that are upsetting to you. The result can be an angry confrontation, even a violent one. "Excuse me," "Pardon me," "I'm sorry," "I was wrong," "That was my fault," and other such phrases convey that you are a courteous person who respects others and takes responsibility for your mistakes. These phrases diffuse rather than provoke anger in others. As the Bible says, "A soft answer turns away wrath (Proverb 15:1)."
- Using phrases such as, "Yes, sir" and "Yes, ma'am," when communicating with an adult conveys that you respect the individual. Why? Because we respect all people.
- You should use courteous words that convey respect when talking to others. Courteous language can win you respect and popularity with others. If you do not understand something someone has said, you can respectfully respond with a phrase like, "Excuse me?" or "Pardon me?" These phrases convey both respect for the person you are speaking with, as well as the idea that you are an intelligent, alert individual. Refrain from using terms like "yea," "uh huh," "yep," "yis," "ya," and other slang words. Slang words convey the idea that you have a poor vocabulary, that you are not very intelligent, or that you are lazy. Speak clearly, especially when speaking

with adults. When you mean yes or no, say yes or no, respectively. Always say what you mean and mean what you say. Carry through on your promises, even if it is a sacrifice. If you do what you say you will do, then you will gain the respect and admiration of others. Also, you will learn to watch what you promise to do. It is better to say no to a request than it is to say yes and not follow through.

- It is important that you use language to help rather than to hurt people.
- You should monitor your words to make sure that what you say is appropriate. "One of the first things a physician says to the patient is, 'Let me see your tongue.' A spiritual advisor might do the same" (N. Adams).
- Teach the negative consequences of gossip.

HOW I PLAN TO TEACH IT (MY METHODS)
- Ask children how they feel when other people use bad words.
- Ask them how they feel when they hear these words in public.
- Ask them why using these words is not appropriate. Ask, "What are some reasons that you can think of for not using these words?"
- Make all the points listed above in terms our children can understand.
- Ask, "Why shouldn't we support movies/TV where people use these words?"
- Play a game: Give each person a piece of paper and have him or her list words we use at our home that build up our family members. Then have them list all the words that are not appropriate because they tear down family members. Also, list those words that show disrespect for members of the family. Then bring out a nice jewelry box and put all the nice (or gem) words in the box. Then bring out a trash can and have everyone throw the bad words (the words that convey disrespect and bring people down) into the trash can. Label the words in the trash can "TRASH words," and make sure everyone sees us put them in the garbage. At this stage in the lesson, ask family members to try their best to not use TRASH or GARBAGE words because they do not belong in our house.
- Make a sign that says, "TRASH words don't belong in our house."

HOW I PLAN TO FIND OUT IF THEY KNOW AND DO WHAT I WANT THEM TO

- Observe how my children speak to their parents, to each other, and to their friends. Ask their friends (in a delicate way) what kind of language my child uses when he or she is not at home.
- Hold one-on-one interviews using the *Progress Tracker* to determine what they know and do about our family's language standards.
- Post a sign that says, "TRASH WORDS don't belong in our house."

HOW I PLAN TO REINFORCE WHAT I HAVE TAUGHT

- Stop and courteously remind the child when he or she uses inappropriate language.
- Use appropriate language instead of profane, vulgar, or crude language in my personal life.
- Avoid using slang (Use discretion here. Sometimes we use slang in fun, and teenagers have their own language that they use amongst themselves for fun).
- Encourage children to refrain from TV, videos, or music where vulgar and profane language is used.
- Every time a child uses an inappropriate word, have him or her write it on a piece of paper and throw it in the trash. Make the point that such words do not belong in our house.

WE BELIEVE IN BEING GRATEFUL

WHAT I WANT THEM TO KNOW

• It is important to be grateful for the things that you receive in life.
• You should express your gratitude often.
• Expressing gratitude will make you and others feel better.
• Expressing gratitude has many advantages.
• There are many ways you can express and demonstrate gratitude.

WHAT I WANT THEM TO DO

• Express gratitude for things that others do for them
• Express gratitude for the things they enjoy in life
• Display a grateful attitude

WHAT I PLAN TO TEACH

• Gratitude is a feeling of thankful appreciation for favors/benefits received.
• Expressing gratitude is something that our family values.
• It is important to feel and express gratitude for the things you have and the things you will receive in the future.
• It is important to express gratitude, even when things are not going well. People who are grateful are much happier than those who are not.
• We have many things we take for granted that we should be grateful for. These include (list all things the family has that can be considered blessings).
• Happiness is not getting more but being grateful for the things you already have in life. When we are not grateful, we cannot enjoy the things we have. Do not put off being grateful until you get the next thing you want, because shortly after you get that thing, you will want something else—which means that you will always be putting off being grateful.

- There are many advantages to consistently expressing gratitude and having a grateful attitude. People like doing nice things for you if you show appreciation and express gratitude for the things that you receive. When you express gratitude on a regular basis, it reminds you of the good things in your life. People who express gratitude become optimistic about life because they see it from the bright side.
- There are many ways to express gratitude. These include saying, "thanks," writing a thank you note, doing something nice for someone who has done something nice for you, helping and serving others, doing the dishes after a good meal, and so on.

HOW I PLAN TO TEACH IT (MY METHODS)

- List things some other people do not have that we enjoy, such as sight, hearing, health, a home, a job, friends, and each other.
- Ask them what things they are grateful for.
- Ask them to name some of the people who made it possible for them to have these things in their life. Ask them for ideas about how they can express gratitude for these things.
- Make the points listed above.
- Show a video that portrays a character with a grateful attitude.
- Read a book about a character with a grateful attitude.
- Read quotes that support these principles about gratitude.

HOW I PLAN TO FIND OUT IF THEY KNOW AND DO WHAT I WANT THEM TO

- Hold one-on-one interviews using *the Progress Tracker* to determine what the children think and do about gratitude.
- Observe their attitudes and behaviors and offer compliments or gentle reminders, as needed.

HOW I PLAN TO REINFORCE WHAT I HAVE TAUGHT

- Model a grateful attitude by expressing appreciation for my blessings daily.
- Read a quote every evening that pertains to some aspect of gratitude.

DEVELOPING AND MAINTAINING SPIRITUALITY

WHAT I WANT THEM TO KNOW

- It is important to develop yourself spiritually, have faith in God, and earnestly strive to do His will in your life.
- There are many things you can do to become a more spiritual person.
- The scriptures provide guidance that you can use as a standard to judge your thoughts and actions.
- There are many benefits to living in accordance with what is outlined in the scriptures.
- There are many disadvantages to not living according to these guidelines.

WHAT I WANT THEM TO DO

- Pray and meditate every morning and every night
- Read at least one page in the scriptures every day
- Attend church on a weekly basis
- Provide voluntary service to others
- Use the scriptures as a standard against which to judge their thoughts and behaviors; live in a manner that is consistent with this standard
- When their behaviors do not conform to the scriptures, make an earnest effort to change by striving to bring them into conformance (repentance)

WHAT I PLAN TO TEACH

- The key to becoming a happy person is to learn to live a balanced life. Developing yourself spiritually is an important part of being balanced.
- According to an unknown author, becoming spiritual requires us to "gain victory over ourselves, and to come into communion with the

infinite (God). Spirituality impels one to conquer difficulties and acquire more and more strength. To feel one's faculties unfolding, and truth expanding in the soul, is one of life's most sublime experiences."

- Considerable scientific and testimonial research indicates there are many benefits to becoming spiritual in a religious context.
- People who are spiritual have the added dimension of understanding that with God, nothing is impossible. They also recognize that although the world we live in is filled with problems, it is also filled with things we need to overcome them.
- Praying, meditating, reading scriptures and inspirational words on a daily basis, striving to live in conformity with the scriptures, working to overcome our weaknesses, and serving others can help us to become more spiritual and to experience joy.
- Attending church can help us to become more spiritual because it puts us in touch with others who are like-minded, provides us with encouragement to improve ourselves, and provides opportunities for service.
- Providing voluntary service to others is a reward in itself.
- Use scripture as a standard against which to judge thoughts and behaviors, and live in a manner that is consistent with this standard.
- When your behaviors do not conform to the scriptures, make an earnest effort to change by striving to bring your actions into conformance. That is, when you do things that are contrary to what is outlined in the scriptures, you should strive to overcome these things by feeling sorrow, confessing, and making restitution. For example, if you are unkind to others, you should feel sad about what you did and do something nice to make those you hurt feel better, such as buying them an ice-cream cone or helping them with their chores. This will make both the offender and the person he or she hurt feel better. Doing something nice for the person you hurt will show that you are really sorry. Most importantly, strive not to be unkind again, because this will undo all that you have done. If you do, however, make the same mistake again, go through the same steps to make up for your mistake. Eventually, you will overcome your tendency to hurt others.

HOW I PLAN TO TEACH IT (MY METHODS)
- Explain the purposes and benefits of becoming spiritual.
- Give an account of how spirituality has helped me in my life.
- Read an inspirational story like "David and Goliath."
- Watch an inspirational movie like "Chariots of Fire."
- Play inspirational music while everyone quietly mediates. After meditating, listen to everyone who wants to share personal feelings about God.
- Memorize a scripture from the Bible.
- Watch a video like *The Ten Commandments* (by Cecil B. Demille), or Disney's *The Prince of Egypt*.
- Assign children independent reading about a religious topic or a famous religious person and have them report back to the family about what they have learned from their readings.
- Demonstrate how to pray and model regular church attendance.
- Plan and participate in a service project, such as visit a friend in a hospital, bake cookies for a neighbor, or write a letter to grandma.

HOW I PLAN TO FIND OUT IF THEY KNOW AND DO WHAT I WANT THEM TO
- Hold one-on-one interviews using the *Progress Tracker* to determine what the children know about spirituality and what they intend to do or are doing about it (in accordance with what is described above).

HOW I PLAN TO REINFORCE WHAT I HAVE TAUGHT
- Model church attendance, personal prayer (by holding daily family prayer), striving to live a life that conforms to the scriptures, admitting and overcoming my mistakes.
- Provide encouragement/support when children follow my example.
- Read and discuss a scripture every night before dinner/bedtime.

WE BELIEVE IN BEING MEDIA LITERATE

WHAT I WANT THEM TO KNOW

- Electronic media, including television and movies, can have a good or bad influence upon you.
- It is important to use discretion when deciding what to watch.
- Your values and behaviors are influenced by what you see and think about.
- You should not depend on those who produce television and movies to decide what is and is not appropriate for you to watch.
- You should not watch movies or TV programs that do not follow family guidelines.
- Watching television can take you away from other activities that you need to be a healthy person.
- Learning the mechanics and artistry involved in creating TV and movies (script, subtext, lighting, music, casting) can help you better appreciate and evaluate this form of entertainment.

WHAT I WANT THEM TO DO

- Be discriminating in the TV and movies they watch, both in terms of quality and quantity
- Avoid TV and movies that promote values not consistent with family values

WHAT I PLAN TO TEACH

- Our family has specific rules regarding watching TV and movies to protect you morally and spiritually.
- What is good about TV and movies? TV can be used to promote positive values and character traits. The media can draw our attention to problems in society and provide ideas about how to

overcome them. The "real" movies, such as documentaries and nature shows, can be educational.

- Many programs sensationalize violence, show sex without consequences, and portray adults who seem to never grow up. These artificial and oftentimes crude depictions of life can convey the idea that violence is an acceptable means of resolving problems, that sex is simply an act of temporary pleasure, that being single is preferable to being married, and that everything is funny when, in fact, just the opposite is true. Most adults do settle down; not everything in life is funny (as is depicted in many sitcoms); not everyone is trim and sexy (nor need they be); marriage and family life are wonderful and much better than the "easy come, easy go" mentality depicted on the big screen.
- Advertisements that attempt to persuade us to buy things we do not need, particularly on credit, can give the false impression that life is a "play now, pay later" proposition
- It is important to be able to distinguish the difference between "real" TV and the kind that portrays life as being full of violence, sex, drugs, and cops. TV programs that depict people getting away with things like sex and violence without depicting the consequences are selling a lie. No matter how well the lie is depicted, it *is* a lie. There are many negative consequences to uncommitted sex, including illegitimate pregnancy, abortion, broken hearts, and sexually transmitted diseases, including HIV/AIDS. In reality, adultery, though often depicted as romantic and commonplace, often leads to divorce, dashed hopes and dreams of children, and a multitude of other problems that can last a lifetime. Every time a <u>real</u> person is killed, family members suffer under the weight of grief, funeral expenses, lost potential income, and on and on. When you watch TV programs and movies that do not show reality, you can develop a false perception of the "real world." Young people who do not have a lot of experience in life may take risks and do things they would not do if they were aware of the many negative consequences associated with the high-risk behavior that is glorified onscreen. They do not realize that even though *we* can choose what to do with our lives, *we* have no choice about consequences.

- TV and movie producers would have us follow their guidance on what to watch. They have produced rating systems to help us monitor our viewing habits; however, if they were truly concerned about our well-being, they would not produce promiscuous and violent movies. Do not trust those who promote violent and irresponsible behavior to give you good guidance on what you should or should not watch. For the most part, their main objective is to make money, and they know that, for better or worse, humans are naturally attracted to sex and violence. Hence, they exploit this human tendency, regardless of the consequences, to make money.
- Establish your own TV or movie rating system.
- There are many important and interesting things you can do instead of watching TV: swim, practice a musical instrument, read a book, roller blade, bake cookies, write a letter or write in your journal, do homework, ride your bike, fly a kite, acquire a hobby like making jewelry or pottery, work on an art project, walk the dog or herd the cat, call a friend, shoot baskets, practice fencing or karate, and so on.
- You can learn how to resist the pressure to watch bad movies.
- You can learn what to do when you are with your friends and a movie you are watching turns out to be a bad one.
- A steady diet of violence can make people insensitive to pain, more aggressive, and inclined to perceive a world full of violence.

HOW I PLAN TO TEACH IT (MY METHODS)
- Discuss ways of rating music, TV, and movies.
- Devise a Family Rating System that is consistent with our family values and sets guidelines for when, how much, and what kinds of entertainment are appropriate for our family members.
- Assign kids to watch, analyze, and report on four commercials.
- Assign them to watch, analyze, and report on two movies.
- Assign them to watch, analyze, and report on two sitcoms.
- Make a video using all the basic elements, including music (CD player for background music) and lighting.
- Put together a newscast (which story comes first, which gets told, from whose perspective), a sitcom, a movie, or documentary. Assign different individuals to write, direct, and produce some form of entertainment that you will later analyze as a family.

- Watch and discuss a video together.
- Watch and discuss a sitcom together. How does the sitcom uphold or go against our family's goals? In many instances, kids talk back to parents, parents are portrayed to be less competent than kids, people are selfish, children are rude to each other, people care more about money than other people, people are dishonest, people have low morals and use crude language.
- Review all points in previous section of the lesson plan.

HOW I PLAN TO FIND OUT IF THEY KNOW AND DO WHAT I WANT THEM TO

- Hold one-on-one interviews using the *Progress Tracker* to determine what they know and plan to do about media literacy.

HOW I PLAN TO REINFORCE WHAT I HAVE TAUGHT

- Set a good example by only partaking in entertainment that supports our family values.

HOW TO CORRELATE AND CALENDAR FAMILY ACTIVITIES

WHAT I WANT THEM TO KNOW
- There are advantages to planning ahead.
- When we plan ahead, things go better.
- We can learn to correlate family activities.

WHAT I WANT THEM TO DO
- Meet with the family on a weekly basis to plan and correlate activities
- Keep a personal calendar (keep on wall for younger children)

WHAT I PLAN TO TEACH
- When we plan ahead, things go better.
- We can plan better activities.
- When we know what is coming up, we can better prepare.
- If we plan ahead and save money, we can participate in exciting family activities, including vacations.
- When we plan ahead, we can avoid last-minute decisions that can be costly and can cause stress and family conflict.
- If we plan ahead, the family can better support you in your individual activities because we will know when and where they are scheduled.
- Each family member should keep a calendar and bring it to our weekly family meeting.
- We will schedule all family activities, school activities, tests and project due dates, etc.

HOW I PLAN TO TEACH IT (MY METHODS)

- Obtain a large "family" calendar that can be hung in a place where everyone can see it.
- Prior to the meeting, calendar all of our upcoming activities, including a weekly family meeting (when we will correlate family activities and teach a lesson). Also, record a time when we plan to have a weekly outing or activity (like every Saturday afternoon, or the first Saturday of the month, or during dinner out as a family on Thursdays).
- Explain the benefits of keeping a calendar.
- Demonstrate how to manage the calendar.
- Give everyone their own calendar and ask them to list their upcoming activities, including the weekly family meeting and activity/outing.

HOW I PLAN TO FIND OUT IF THEY KNOW AND DO WHAT I WANT THEM TO

- Observe at every weekly family meeting whether or not children are keeping their calendars current.
- Hold one-on-one interviews using the *Progress Tracker* to determine if children need help in keeping their calendars current.

HOW I PLAN TO REINFORCE WHAT I HAVE TAUGHT

- Post a family calendar and refer to it every evening to remind everyone what is coming up the next day.
- Set an example by keeping my own calendar current.
- Reward children when they come to family meetings with their calendar current.

SAMPLE LESSON PLAN #9

WE BELIEVE IN SETTING GOALS

WHAT I WANT THEM TO KNOW
- Setting goals can help you accomplish things that you would not otherwise accomplish.
- Achieving goals can help improve your self-esteem.
- You must have action plans to achieve your goals.
- Goals should be specific.
- Goals should be written down.
- Goals should be realistic.
- Goals should be stated in terms of a specific time period.
- Goals should be directed toward accomplishing good things in your life.
- You should review your goals on a regular basis.

WHAT I WANT THEM TO DO
- Write goals in their journal that describe what they want to accomplish this month, this year, in the next five years, and before they graduate from high school
- Write what action steps they will need to take to accomplish each goal
- Read their goals once a week and record progress. List any additional action steps they may need to take to accomplish their goals, and write down any new goals

WHAT I PLAN TO TEACH
- Goals are written statements that explain what you want to obtain or accomplish within a certain period of time.
- Action plans are those specific things you plan to do to achieve your goals.
- Setting goals can help you accomplish things that you would not otherwise accomplish.

- Achieving goals can help improve the way you feel about yourself.
- Goals should be specific and written down. Goals should be realistic and be stated in terms of a specific time period. To ensure that your goals will lead you to accomplishing good things in life, you should regularly review your goals and adjust them, as needed.
- Write goals in your journal that describe what you want to accomplish this month, this year, in the next five years, and before you graduate from high school. Then write what action steps you will need to take to accomplish your goals.
- Review your goals once a week. At this time you should record progress toward your goals, list any additional action steps you may need to take to accomplish your goals, and write down any new goals.

HOW I PLAN TO TEACH IT (MY METHODS)
- Ask children what goals are and why goal-setting is important.
- Ask them if they have ever set goals and, if so, whether or not they achieved them.
- Ask them what must be done to achieve goals.
- As per above, explain what goals and action plans are, why they are important, and how to write them down.
- Tell a story, read a book, or show a video that depicts someone who benefited from setting goals.
- Show the children my goals and action plans. Tell them about some of the goals I have set and accomplished and what I had to do to achieve them.
- Use the following format to teach children how to write goals and action plans:
    - What I Want To Accomplish/Obtain
    - (My Goals)
    - How I Plan To Accomplish/Obtain This
    - (My Action Plans)
- Help each child write down a goal he or she can accomplish in the next week, along with the action plans required to reach the goal.
- Assign children to report on their goal at the next family meeting.
- Help each child write down a long-term goal and the action plans required to accomplish it.

HOW I PLAN TO FIND OUT IF THEY KNOW AND DO WHAT I WANT THEM TO

• Hold one-on-one interviews using the *Progress Tracker* to determine what they know about goal-setting and writing action plans and what they are doing to accomplish their goals.

HOW I PLAN TO REINFORCE WHAT I HAVE TAUGHT

• Set and report on my personal goals.
• Set family goals and write action plans.
• Review status of family goals in weekly family meeting.
• At the beginning of every year, hold a special family meeting to set our family goals for the year.

WE BELIEVE IN SHOWING KINDNESS TO EVERYONE

WHAT I WANT THEM TO KNOW
- Kindness is treating others in a nice way.
- Kindness is an important family value.
- We should be kind to everyone, even people who are mean to us.

WHAT I WANT THEM TO DO
- Practice being kind to others
- Treat others the way they want to be treated
- Encourage other people instead of tearing them down
- Repeat the good things instead of the bad things they know about other people

WHAT I PLAN TO TEACH
- Kindness is treating other people in a nice way by saying nice things to them and doing nice things for them.
- You should practice being kind to everyone, even those people who are not kind to you.
- If someone yells at you, answer him or her in a soft voice. If you yell back, it will only make matters worse.
- When others get to know you, they will treat you like you treat them. Therefore, if you treat other people with kindness, others will eventually treat you the same way. You will have a lot more friends when you practice kindness, because people like to be around kind people.
- Do not think bad things about other people. Even if they are mean to you, think to yourself, "She must be having a bad day, week, month or year" or "He must be feeling weak today" because

rudeness is a weak person's imitation of strength. When you are rude, you are weak, and it does not feel good to be weak.
- When you talk about other people, mention their good points instead of their weaknesses.
- Learn to say kind things to people. Always build people up instead of tearing them down. Never call people names that can hurt their feelings.
- The best way to show kindness is to do nice things for people even when they do not ask you to.
- Take the time to listen carefully when other people talk to you. This is a great way to show you care.

HOW I PLAN TO TEACH IT (MY METHODS)
- Ask everyone for ideas about what they think kindness is.
- Ask how they feel when people treat them rudely. Ask, "Would you rather be around rude people or kind people?" Ask them how they feel when people are kind to them.
- During our family meeting, ask everyone to write down something nice about everyone else in the family. Then read the responses aloud. Ask how they felt when they heard nice things about themselves
- Explain points made above.
- Make a list of kind words.
- Role-play responding in a kind way to someone who is not kind.
- Write every child a note and tell him or her how great you think he or he is.
- Do a chore for every child and follow up by saying, "I did a kind thing for you today because I love you."
- Post a sign that says, "Our Family Believes in Random Acts of Kindness."

HOW I PLAN TO FIND OUT IF THEY KNOW AND DO WHAT I WANT THEM TO
- Observe how family members treat one another, whether or not they use kind words and do kind deeds,
- Hold one-on-one interviews using the *Progress Tracker* to determine what they know about the importance of kindness and what they are doing about it.

HOW I PLAN TO REINFORCE WHAT I HAVE TAUGHT

• Model kindness in my daily activities.

• Do something nice for the children when they are not expecting it.

• Leave notes expressing love and appreciation.

• Buy treats or things they like, for no reason at all. (Although gifts are often expected on birthdays and many holidays, they are not expected because a person smiled or said something nice. We will give small gifts and say nice things when the children least expect it.)

- How do think the horse felt about receiving treatment?
- How do you know the horse owner cared about the horse?
- If we compare your disobedience to Dakota's attempts to avoid treatment, how might the actions taken to treat the horse be compared to the actions I take when you are unwilling to cooperate with my rules and requests?
- When I take time to correct you, even if you do not want to be corrected, what does that say about my feelings about you?

• Listen to the following hypothetical situation and answer the questions to determine how it relates to discipline.
- Imagine walking home from school. You see your little brother playing ball   in the front yard. The ball goes into the street. You also see a truck coming   down the street while your brother starts toward the ball.
  1. What would you do?
  2. What would you say to him after the truck passed?
  3. What if he became angry with you for correcting him?
  4. How might we misunderstand our parents when they try to correct us?

• When someone illuminates the fact that you are doing something wrong, be humble and thank him or her. Do not hold a grudge. It is true that some people do not correct people in a spirit of love. Forgive them anyway.
• We understand that everyone makes mistakes. However, we should strive to learn from and overcome our faults.

HOW I PLAN TO TEACH IT (MY METHODS)
• Define discipline and explain when and why it will be applied in our family.
• Discuss how society applies discipline, and for what reasons.
• Ask the above questions before and after I read the story to determine how the children initially look at discipline and how they feel about it after the story.
• Repeat the explanation of why we apply discipline.
• Encourage them to be humble and realize that discipline is an act of love designed to help rather than hurt them.

- Review the family rules, the purpose of having family rules, and the types of discipline that will be applied if the rules are violated. Also note that discipline will not be applied until parents have had time to hear what happened and to think about what form of discipline best fits the infraction.
- Show a video that reinforces the benefits of correct discipline.

HOW I PLAN TO FIND OUT IF THEY KNOW AND DO WHAT I WANT THEM TO
- Observe how well each child adheres to rules and accepts discipline.
- Hold one-on-one interviews using the *Progress Tracker* to determine if children understand the rules and the corresponding consequences and if they are willing to abide by the rules and humbly accept correction.

HOW I PLAN TO REINFORCE WHAT I HAVE TAUGHT
- Model loving discipline by not disciplining until I know all the facts.
- When I make mistakes or am corrected by someone, I will accept the correction with a good attitude.
- Occasionally tell stories about how discipline can help people improve.

DEVELOPING PROPER GROOMING HABITS

WHAT I WANT THEM TO KNOW
- People judge you and treat you a certain way based on your physical appearance and hygiene.
- It is important to be your "best self" by keeping yourself clean, well-dressed, and in good mental and physical condition.

WHAT I WANT THEM TO DO
- Adopt and practice good grooming habits

WHAT I PLAN TO TEACH
- Other people judge you based on your appearance and your personal hygiene.
- If you dress in a neat and comely manner, people (particularly adults) tend to show you more respect.
- You should develop a habit of good grooming by adopting the following habits: 1) maintain good posture, 2) shower or bathe every day, 3) wash your hair at least every other day, 4) wash your entire body with soap, 5) wear deodorant (as a teenager), 6) keep your nails clean and trim, 7) avoid nail-biting, 8) keep your hair trim and neat, 9) keep your leather shoes polished, 10) keep your clothes in good repair (buttons sewed on, tears promptly repaired, generally clean and neat), 11) brush your teeth morning and night, 12) floss your teeth daily, 13) get sufficient exercise, and 14) eat a healthy diet so you can keep your weight at a desirable level.

HOW I PLAN TO TEACH IT (MY METHODS)

- Explain what good grooming is, why it is important, and what we want the children/teenagers to do about it.
- Put together a grooming checklist to hang in the bathroom.
- Show a video that explains the benefits of good grooming and demonstrates examples of good grooming.

HOW I PLAN TO FIND OUT IF THEY KNOW AND DO WHAT I WANT THEM TO

- Observe whether or not children are practicing good grooming habits.
- Hold one-on-one interviews using the *Progress Tracker* to determine what they know and what they are doing about good grooming habits.

HOW I PLAN TO REINFORCE WHAT I HAVE TAUGHT

- Set an example of good grooming.
- Compliment children when they are well-groomed.
- Conduct follow-up lessons on the importance of good grooming.

RECOGNIZING AND MANAGING STRESS

WHAT I WANT THEM TO KNOW
- Stress is the strain we feel when things happen to us.
- It is important to understand stress so we can manage it.
- We can learn strategies to help us manage, and sometimes even avoid, stress.

WHAT I WANT THEM TO DO
- Learn to recognize stress
- Learn to avoid unnecessary stress triggers
- Learn to manage stress
- Take actions that lessen the negative effects of stress

WHAT I PLAN TO TEACH
- Stress is the strain we feel when negative or positive things happen to us.
- Some stress is unavoidable, like an increased workload at school, serious personal injury, changes in school or living conditions, a flat tire on your bike or car, and/or the death of a pet, friend, or family member.
- Stress can be either beneficial or harmful, depending on how we prepare for and deal with it.
- A little stress can be good. For example, before we play an important game, take a test, participate in a recital, or act in a play, we may feel stress that helps us adapt to the situation by increasing our mental and physical alertness.
- Although moderate amounts of stress can be helpful, extreme amounts of stress can harm both our bodies and our minds. This is

particularly true when we are under extreme stress for a sustained period of time. Under extreme stress, we can become overwhelmed, and our ability to perform even simple tasks can be compromised.

- We can take steps to avoid extreme stress. For example, we can fortify ourselves against stress by living balanced lives. People who exercise, eat good food, get adequate sleep, engage in spiritual activities, feel good about themselves, and so on, are better able to deal with stress. If you prepare yourself to accomplish your goals, you will more likely succeed and suffer less stress when the opportunities you desire present themselves. For example, if you want to be a famous singer and you never practice singing until a few days before you have an audition, you will feel a lot of stress and probably not perform at your best, which may prevent you from reaching your goal. If you do not study for a test until the night before, taking the test may be a very stressful experience. The stress connected with this test could have been avoided if you had studied for an hour each day rather than trying to cram the night before. If you hope to win a track meet and you do not practice, you will lack the confidence and stamina to do your best.

- Negative things that can cause stress include a poor diet, not being prepared for a test, getting yelled at by a parent or teacher, lacking confidence in your ability to do something you must do (like sing a solo), and irresponsible behavior in general.

- You can avoid stress to a great extent if you are/become a responsible and a self-disciplined person.

- Some things you can do to manage stress include the following: 1) better prepare for whatever task you find difficult, 2) review your school subjects every night whether or not you have homework, 3) be kind to others because others will likely treat you as you treat them, 4) get up earlier so you are not rushed when getting ready for school, 5) pray daily, asking for help when you need it, 6) read books or watch movies about how to overcome or to manage stress, 7) relax and talk positively when you feel stress, 8) live a balanced life, 9) keep a journal and record your frustrations or work out a plan to overcome them, 10) do what you say you will do, 11) tackle hard tasks first, then focus on less important tasks, 12) do not over-commit yourself and, if you do, enlist the help of others to get everything done, and 13) serve others.

HOW I PLAN TO TEACH IT (MY METHODS)

• Explain what stress is.
• Ask what causes stress.
• Ask what can be done prevent stress.
• Ask what can be done to manage stress.
• Have children list the things they can change in their lives to reduce stress.
• Present ideas on how to reduce stress and how to prevent the negative mental and physical effects of stress.
• Listen to a tape on how to relax.

HOW I PLAN TO FIND OUT IF THEY KNOW AND DO WHAT I WANT THEM TO

• Set a good personal example of how to reduce and manage stress.
• Hold one-on-one interviews using the *Progress Tracker* to determine what each child is doing to reduce and manage stress.

HOW I PLAN TO REINFORCE WHAT I HAVE TAUGHT

• Put up a poster that lists all the ways our family can avoid stress. Refer to the poster throughout the week.
• Compliment children when I observe them doing things that reduce stress.
• Watch a video that talks about how to relax.
• Listen to a CD about managing stress.
• Turn off television on Sundays and listen to relaxing music.

UNDERSTAND THAT WE ARE WHAT WE EAT

WHAT I WANT THEM TO KNOW
• Eating a balanced diet can help you look, feel, and function better.

WHAT I WANT THEM TO DO
• Eat a low-fat and high-fiber diet
• Limit foods and beverages that are high in calories and low in nutrients

WHAT I PLAN TO TEACH
• The USDA Food Pyramid and the U.S. Dietary Guidelines help us choose healthy foods in the appropriate portions.
• Eating a low-fat diet can help you maintain a healthy weight, become more socially acceptable, feel better about yourself and the way you look, have more energy, and have more fun. Strive to eat less than 25 grams of fat per day.
• Eating foods that are high in fiber helps regulate your body's metabolism, improves digestion, and helps prevent disease. Strive to eat more than 12 grams of fiber each day.
• Drink at least six 8-ounce glasses of liquid every day, preferably water and milk.
• Limit the candy and carbonated beverages you consume because they are high in calories and low in nutrients.
• Do not drink caffeinated beverages, including caffeinated tea and soda pop.

HOW I PLAN TO TEACH IT (MY METHODS)
• Display and explain the USDA Food Pyramid and U.S. Dietary Guidelines.
• Lecture on the importance of eating low-fat and high-fiber foods.

- Provide each family member a list of low-fat and high-fiber foods.
- Demonstrate how to determine the amount of fat and fiber in different foods (note, use the Weight Watcher's guide at http://www.weightwatchers.com).
- List high-calorie/low-nutrient foods. Discuss ways of limiting these foods.
- Help children list their favorite low-fat and high-fiber foods, and write a plan that they will follow for one week to track how many fat and fiber grams they consume each day. Also, have them set a goal for limiting the number of high-calorie/low-nutrient foods they eat over the coming week.
- Serve low-fat/high-fiber foods and ask children to estimate the number of fat and fiber grams in each serving.
- Visibly post in the kitchen the USDA Food Pyramid and the U.S. Dietary Guidelines.

HOW I PLAN TO FIND OUT IF THEY KNOW AND DO WHAT I WANT THEM TO
- At the next meeting, have children report on their progress.
- Hold one-on-one interviews using the *Progress Tracker* to determine if children are eating low-fat/high-fiber foods.

HOW I PLAN TO REINFORCE WHAT I HAVE TAUGHT
- Refer children to the USDA Food Pyramid and the U.S. Dietary Guidelines posted in the kitchen.
- Serve favorite low-fat and high-fiber foods.
- Develop your own personal examples.

HOW TO GET AND KEEP POSITIVE SELF-ESTEEM

WHAT I WANT THEM TO KNOW

- Some people think they are better than others. A person with a high self-esteem actually shows respect to other people rather than acting superior toward them.
- Many people think they are not as good as others when, in fact, each and every person is of great worth and deserves to be treated with respect.
- It is important that you have high self-esteem.
- You can do specific things to ensure that you gain and maintain high self-esteem.

WHAT I WANT THEM TO DO

- Strive to attain and maintain high self-esteem throughout their lives
- Love themselves

WHAT I PLAN TO TEACH

- Self-esteem is how good you feel about yourself.
- People who have high self-esteem feel good about themselves. They like themselves. They feel a sense of accomplishment in their lives. They recognize their talents and abilities and use them to improve their lives and the lives of others. They believe life is good in spite of the problems they must face. They do better in school and work and have more confidence in their personal abilities. They are typically more successful than those who do not have high self-esteem.
- When you are young, the way you feel about yourself has a lot to do with what other people have said to you. Parents and peers can either send positive or negative messages that help you create

your perception of who you think you are and how good you are. Unfortunately, many people are exposed to a lot of bad messages from insensitive people, and they develop a low self-esteem. This is unfortunate, because everyone who has ever been born on this earth has worth and value. Therefore, everyone should and can learn to develop high self-esteem that can help him or her become a happy and successful person.

- As you strive to develop high self-esteem, always remember that you are a person of great worth, that you are unique, and that you have many things you can contribute to society (regardless of your circumstances). Also, learn to set realistic goals and then set a plan for reaching them. People who consistently accomplish goals in their lives have a tendency to feel better about themselves.

- Strive to say what you mean and mean what you say. That is, if you tell someone you will do something for him or her, then do it.

- Live a balanced life. If you eat right, exercise regularly, and get adequate rest, you will look better and feel better about yourself.

- When you talk to yourself (which we all do in our minds) say mostly good things. It is okay to be upset with yourself when you do not do what you know you should. However, at the same time, if you are upset with yourself, you should assure yourself that you will do better next time, and then think about ways of avoiding the same mistake. We are all "works in progress." No one is perfect. We all make mistakes. What is important is that we work on our weaknesses. If we do, we will eventually overcome them. (Cognitive Behavioral Therapy is good here.)

- Some threats to your self-esteem include hanging around people who always put you down and doing what others want you to do instead of doing what you feel is best.

- People who do things that go against their personal values can develop low self-esteem. To avoid this, you could keep a journal that lists how you feel about things that are important to you. Read it often to remind yourself of your goals and ideals. This will help you "watch yourself," so you can avoid doing things that will make you feel bad. This can also help you make decisions about what you should and should not do with your life. For example, if you believe it is wrong to be unkind to other people but you are unkind to your family, then you will feel guilt and this can cause you to feel bad about yourself. Likewise, if you feel like people should not steal or lie but you steal or lie a lot, you will begin to feel bad about yourself. The point here is to watch yourself. If you start to do something and you get an "uh oh" feeling, do not repeat the bad behavior. Feelings of guilt and disappointment help you recognize that what you are doing may not be right.

- You can learn to neutralize and process negative messages in a positive way; this is called cognitive restructuring. For example, if you really like playing the guitar and someone overhears you practicing and makes the comment, "You're not that great," say to yourself, "Not yet." If someone says to you, "Gee, you're dumb," say to yourself, "Not when I study."
- To overcome bad feelings that result when you do things you should not, be determined to "bounce back" and do better the next time. If you have hurt someone, ask for forgiveness. Read your journal often as a constant reminder of what is important to you.
- Commit yourself to work on developing high self-esteem and avoiding those things that can make you feel bad about yourself.

HOW I PLAN TO TEACH IT (MY METHODS)
- Ask, "What is self-esteem?" After fielding a few responses, explain what it is.
- Ask family members to close their eyes and imagine (using the visualization method) that they are looking in the mirror. Ask them to think about how they feel about the person they see in the mirror. "Do you believe this is a nice person, a good person, a talented person, a friendly person? Do you like this person?"
- Ask everyone to write down something nice about everyone else in the family. Collect the lists and read the nice things aloud. Make the point that we can influence how others feel about themselves. Because of this, we should say things to support and encourage one another rather than say cutting and discouraging things.
- Ask, "What helps a person have high self-esteem?"
- Ask, "What makes a person feel bad about him or herself?"
- Role-play cognitive restructuring by having one person make a negative comment and the other explaining out loud how he or she can restructure the comment to diffuse it.

- Ask what can be done to develop high self-esteem.
- Ask what can cause us to have low self-esteem.
- Explain the benefits of high self-esteem and the problems of low self-esteem.
- Ask for ideas about how they can overcome forces that diminish self-esteem.
- Explain what they can do to gain and maintain high self-esteem: set goals and reach goals, live in accordance with their values, be kind to others ("what goes around comes around"), serve others, etc.
- Explain how they can avoid or overcome things that can diminish their self-esteem.
- Have them list things that are important to them: kindness, helpfulness, exercise, getting good grades, playing the piano, getting along with other people. Explain that it is important to live in a way that is consistent with their values (those things that are important to them) to avoid having low self-esteem. Encourage them to place the things they have written in a journal and refer to them often.

HOW I PLAN TO FIND OUT IF THEY KNOW AND DO WHAT I WANT THEM TO
- Observe their attitude and behavior.
- Hold one-on-one interviews using the *Progress Tracker* to determine how they feel about themselves. Also determine whether or not they are consistently striving to improve their self-esteem, encourage positive self-esteem among others, and avoid things that can threaten their self-esteem.

HOW I PLAN TO REINFORCE WHAT I HAVE TAUGHT
- Post a sign that lists the nice things others say about each individual family member (add those things that were listed during the lesson activity).
- Ask family members to add to this sign as they think of or observe good things about other family members. (For example, Jordan is good on his roller blades, is very responsible about doing his chores, loves to help his mom and dad to work around the house, and does well in school.)

SAMPLE LESSON PLAN #16

DEVELOPING STRATEGIES TO RESIST PEER PRESSURE

WHAT I WANT THEM TO KNOW
• Peers will tempt you to do things that are wrong and even dangerous.
• You can learn to resist negative pressure.

WHAT I WANT THEM TO DO
• Practice and learn skills to resist negative pressure as a way to preserve family standards of ethics, health, and safety

WHAT I PLAN TO TEACH
What it is:
• People your own age place pressure on you to do what they want you to do, regardless of the consequences.
• Sometimes your friends or someone your age will pressure you to do inappropriate things because they are having fun and want you to have fun. Oftentimes, however, they pressure you because they do not feel good about something they are doing and want others to do the same thing, supposing that if a lot of people do it, then "it's not so bad." Many times, the reason these individuals do not feel good about the things they are pressuring you to do is because they are insecure about something. For example, they may feel like it is dangerous or unlawful.
• Pressure tactics include begging you, calling you names, or rejecting you (saying they will not be your friend) if you will not do what they want you to do.
• Sometimes peer pressure makes you feel so bad that you are tempted to give in and do what others want you to do, instead of what you want to do.

Why it is important:

• If you give in and do what others want you to do instead of what you think you should do, you become unhappy/confused.

• Therefore, you need to learn how to resist pressure to do things you do not really want to do.

There are a number of benefits to knowing how to resist pressure:

• If you learn to resist pressure to do what others want you to do, you will become a strong, self-directed, mature person. Mature people are those who make up their own mind about things and are not afraid to tell others how they feel. They are in control of their lives. They are cool.

• You should commit to not following along and doing things that can hurt you or that you may feel bad about later.

• These skills may help you avoid embarrassment.

• They can help you look intelligent.

• You will become a leader because people your age like other people who can stand up to pressure. They will want to follow you because they feel safe and supported in their decisions to not give in to pressure from others.

The disadvantages of not knowing how to resist pressure:

• You may not know what to say when others try to change your mind.

• If you do not learn these skills, you may give into pressure and become insecure.

• You may be embarrassed in front of friends when you could have avoided this and looked and sounded cool in your response.

• You become a follower instead of a leader.

What you should do about it:

• When people pressure you to do things you do not really want to do, you can: 1) say no and mean it, 2) use a comeback, 3) reverse the pressure, or 4) leave the place where you are being pressured.

    – SAY NO...

    "Just say no" works when 1) you say no like you mean it, and 2) you say it with an assertive voice and body language.

    – COMEBACKS...

    If the person who is pressuring you will not take no for an answer, do not give long explanations, just say something like,

"Lighten up, dude/girl," "Read my lips, **no**," or "Which part of the word **no** don't you understand?" Other ways of saying no include, "Get off my back," "Get a life," "Don't you have anything better to do than bother me?" or "Get lost."

– REVERSE THE PRESSURE COMEBACKS…

Ask these types of questions: "Why do you feel like you need to convince people to go along with you?" "What makes you think that your ideas are better than everyone else's?" "Do you think the world revolves around your thoughts?" "Why can't you just let other people do their own thing?" "Don't you think people that go around trying to get everyone else to do what they want are pushy?" "Why are you so pushy?" "Don't you think people who can have fun without drinking are more mature than those who have to drink to have a good time?" "Why do you have to drink to have fun? Are you addicted?" OR "Are you practicing your speech on me? Practice on someone else."

– Exit the situation…

If all else fails, say something like, "I'm outta here," or "This isn't fun. I'm gone." Some kids get so embarrassed by pressure that they give into it and lose their lives. You can overcome embarrassment, but you cannot overcome the consequences of giving into something that can hurt or kill you. Don't die of embarrassment (literally).

Commitment:

Will you commit to learning and practicing comebacks?

HOW I PLAN TO TEACH IT

• Lecture to explain what negative peer pressure is and why it is important to learn to resist it.
• Ask children what kinds of peer pressure they have witnessed or experienced and get their ideas for resisting pressure.
• Demonstrate how to use comebacks.
• Role-play to allow children to practice comebacks.
• Use directed independent learning by assigning kids to pretend some of their friends are pressuring them to use alcohol. Have them come up with their own comebacks and practice them for the next

family meeting when you or others in the family will try to tempt them to give in.
- Post a sign in kitchen that lists the four things kids can do to resist peer pressure.

HOW I PLAN TO FIND OUT IF THEY KNOW AND DO WHAT I WANT THEM TO
- After teaching the entire lesson, have a follow-up session where each child will have a chance to practice resisting pressure to drink alcohol.
- Ask children to report on successes in resisting pressure.
- Hold one-on-one interviews using the *Progress Tracker* to determine how well children are resisting peer pressure.

HOW I PLAN TO REINFORCE WHAT I HAVE TAUGHT
- Make favorable (genuine) comments when the children practice their skills during the follow-up lesson.
- Post a sign in kitchen that lists the four ways of resisting pressure.

PREVENTING DRUG USE

WHAT I WANT THEM TO KNOW
- Using alcohol and other drugs can be harmful and result in many negative consequences.
- You do not need to use alcohol and other drugs to be happy or popular among your friends.

WHAT I WANT THEM TO DO
- Practice encouraging others not to drink alcohol or use other drugs
- Practice resisting pressure to use alcohol and other drugs

WHAT I PLAN TO TEACH
- Alcohol is a drug that alters the way you think and feel, as well as your ability to do things.
- Alcohol is called a depressant because it slows your body down.
- Using alcohol causes people to do things they would not otherwise do, like take dangerous risks.
- Abstaining from alcohol and other drugs can prevent many problems: health conditions, embarrassment, car accidents, unwanted sexual relations and pregnancy, and/or a bad reputation as a result of saying or doing things you would not normally do.
- Explain why people think they need alcohol when in fact they do not.

HOW I PLAN TO TEACH IT (MY METHODS)
- Lecture about alcohol and its negative physical effects.
- Ask children to add their ideas about some of these negative effects.
- Ask children why people drink if there are so many negative effects.
- Role-play resisting pressure to use alcohol with the following comeback strategies:

   THE "I DON'T NEED TO DRINK ALCOHOL" COME-BACK STRATEGY...

- When someone tries to get you to drink for any reason, say, "I don't need to drink." Consider the example below;

     ("Pressurer" says) "Take a drink."

     (You say) "No!"

     (Pressurer says) "Come on, it will help you have a good time."

     (You say) "I don't NEED to drink to have a good time. Besides, alcohol is a depressant. I'm not here to get depressed. I came to have a good time."

     (Pressurer says) "Come on, take a drink; it will help you loosen up."

     (You say) "I don't NEED alcohol to loosen up."

     (Pressurer says) "Come on, take a drink, it will help you feel better."

     (You say) "I don't NEED a drug to feel better. I'll feel better when you're gone."

     REVERSE THE PRESSURE by asking questions like the following: "Why do you feel like you need to convince people to go along with what you want them to do?" "What makes you think that your ideas are better than everyone else's?" "Do you think the world revolves around your perspective?" "Why can't you just let other people do their own thing?" "Don't you think people who go around trying to get everyone else to do what they want are pushy?" "Why are you so pushy?" "Don't you think people who can have fun without drinking are more mature than those who have to drink to have a good time?" "Why do you have to drink to have fun?" OR "Are you addicted?"

- Ask children to sign a contract or make a formal commitment not to drink.

HOW I PLAN TO FIND OUT IF THEY KNOW AND DO WHAT I WANT THEM TO

- Observe their role-playing to determine if they have adopted good comeback strategies.
- Ask them how they feel about drinking.
- Hold one-on-one interviews using the *Progress Tracker* to determine if they feel confident in their ability to resist drugs and alcohol.

HOW I PLAN TO REINFORCE WHAT I HAVE TAUGHT

- Set a good example by not partaking in alcohol or illicit drugs.
- Point out the negative consequences of these substances whenever they become apparent in the media.

DELAYING SEX UNTIL MARRIAGE

WHAT I WANT THEM TO KNOW
- Your parents want you to delay sexual relations until you are married.
- If you commit yourselves and learn the skills needed to delay sex, you will be successful.
- Delaying sexual relations until marriage is consistent with our family values.
- You should realize the connection between thoughts, actions, and certain stimuli. For example, certain music and movies can provoke sexual thoughts that can tempt you to engage in sexual relations.
- Your parents want you to date, to get married, and to have babies, in that order.
- Sex is NOT bad in and of itself. But engaging in premarital sex is a bad choice that is not consistent with our family values.
- Premarital sex has emotional and physical consequences.

WHAT I WANT THEM TO DO
- Take precautions against engaging in sex before marriage
- Refrain from sexual relations until married

WHAT I PLAN TO TEACH
What it is:
- Sexual relations include any kind of physical contact with another person that stimulates them sexually (i.e., passionate kissing, touching private parts, and sexual intercourse).
- If you refrain from sexual relations until marriage, you will have many advantages: you will have more time to 1) learn the relationship skills required to get along with others without sex, 2) test the love expressed by another person, 3) understand personal sexual motives,

4) learn to discern sexual motives and avoid sexual exploitation, 5) learn to recognize and avoid risky situations and safely escape from risky situations, 6) learn how to refute peer pressure, and 7) learn to control urges and to govern sexual thoughts and emotions.

- There are disadvantages of not knowing or doing. If you do engage in sexual relations before marriage, you run a greater risk of acquiring an STD (namely, HIV), becoming pregnant or causing a pregnancy, and/or performing poorly in school—or dropping out of school due to infection or pregnancy.

What you should do about it:

- Do not watch movies or listen to songs that tempt you to be sexual.
- Do not read pornography or visit pornography sites on the Internet.
- Do not entertain sexual thoughts.
- Do not start dating until you are at least 16, and then only date in groups.
- Do not date just one person until you are at least 18 years old.
- If you are having problems, talk to your parents or your religious leader.
- Formally commit (with a behavioral contract) to delay sexual relations until marriage.

HOW I PLAN TO TEACH IT (MY METHODS)

- Lecture briefly on what sex is and what our family values are concerning sexual activity.
- Ask children to give ideas about advantages of delaying and disadvantages of not waiting.
- Read list of advantages of delaying sex until marriage.
- Every child signs a contract to abstain and lists the advantages of abstaining.

HOW I PLAN TO FIND OUT IF THEY KNOW AND DO WHAT I WANT THEM TO

- Have a follow-up session to review abstinence contracts.
- Hold one-on-one interviews using the *Progress Tracker* to determine if children are facing any temptations with sexual intimacy.

HOW I PLAN TO POSITIVELY REINFORCE WHAT I HAVE TAUGHT

- Give a personal example such as explaining why you are committed to fidelity in your marriage.
- Share with the children videos and brochures that reinforce abstinence.
- Share testimonials from positive role models.

LEARNING AND PRACTICING SELF-CONTROL

WHAT I WANT THEM TO KNOW
- You can learn to control themselves.
- You can resist impulses.
- You can resist pressure from others.

WHAT I WANT THEM TO DO
- Delay gratification
- Consciously strive to develop self-control
- Control thoughts and actions

WHAT I WILL TEACH

What it is:
- Self-control is intentionally asserting control over your thoughts and actions to prevent yourself from thinking and doing things that are beyond your familial and personal limits.
- If you practice, you can learn to control the way you talk, the way you look, the way you treat others, the way you dress, your situation in life, the environments you are in (at least to some extent), your motives, your standards, the way you think (remember that thoughts trigger actions), your urges, your behavior, and YOUR LIFE!

RELEVANT QUOTES:

"A simple reality which is ignored at a terrible price is that most human misery can be prevented by wise and disciplined living." (Victor Brown)

"The breakdown of sexual self-control is a big factor in many of the sex-related problems that plague our society, including: rape, sexual promiscuity, pornography, addiction to sex, sexual harassment, the sexual abuse of children, sexual infidelity in marriage, and the serious damage to families many of these problems cause." (Thomas Likona)

"You can't do wrong and feel right, it's impossible." (Ezra Taft Benson)

SOME PROBLEMS that can arise if you do not have self-control:

- EXAMPLE 1: Some people never learn to control themselves. Therefore, even though they get older, they never become responsible. This causes all kinds of problems. For example, some people never learn to control how much they eat. As a result, they eat more food than they need (or the wrong kinds of food) and they become overweight. This does not make them bad people, but it can cause them many problems. For instance, they are not as socially acceptable; they cannot participate in activities that require a person to be in good physical condition; they do not have as much energy; they do not feel good about themselves; and they can have health problems that result from being overweight.
- EXAMPLE 2: Some people never learn to control their thoughts. This is a problem because they do not learn to concentrate on what they are doing. For example, if you are in school and you do not control what you are thinking about, you will not be able to concentrate on what your teacher is saying. This will prevent you from learning what is being taught, and you will not do as well as you could do in your schoolwork.
- EXAMPLE 3 (Invent another example that applies to our family):
• People who are out of control overeat, oversleep, do not study, scream at others, hit others, shoot others, drink and drive, get in car accidents, and so on. If the people in a society are out of control, the society itself is out of control.

SOME OF THE BENEFITS of having self-control:

• Those who learn to practice self-control are responsible.

• People who are in control of themselves are free to do whatever they choose; those who are out of control are imprisoned by their habits. People who are in control make better students, athletes, artists, teachers, employees, and managers.

• It is not always easy or fun to be in control, but it is worth it.

• It is not much fun to practice playing a musical instrument every day, but it is fun to be able to play music. It is not easy to lift weights or work out every day, but it is worth it to be strong and have an attractive body. It is not that much fun to study, but it is fun to get good grades. It is fun to be in control. If you are in control, you can do anything you decide you truly want to do.

• Not everything that is worthwhile is easy or fun.

• Because your thoughts and feelings (impulses) precede your actions, learn to control your thoughts. If you have an impulse to do something that you know you should not do, redirect your thinking to something else. Learn a song or memorize a poem, or exercise, or do something that takes your mind off what you know you should not do.

• Put first things first. That is, practice doing hard things before easy ones. For example, do your homework or your chores before you go out to play with your friends. Do not give yourself permission to do fun things until you have taken care of your responsibilities.

• Remind yourself that it is not easy, but it is fun, to be in control.

• Ignore others who tempt you to do things you do not want to do.

• Avoid influences that tempt you to do what you should not or prevent you from doing what you should. For example, do not watch television programs or movies, or listen to music, that tempt you or cause you to think thoughts that lead you astray.

• Do watch TV, read books, and attend activities that encourage you to do the things you want to do.

HOW I WILL TEACH IT (MY METHODS)

• Find out what the children already know by asking questions.

• After I find out, I will describe what I think self-control is.

• Ask one child to read a related quote.

- Ask children what problems can arise if people do not have self-control.
- Relate examples of these problems.
- Ask what the benefits of self-control are.
- Show a video clip of a person exercising self-control. For example, I could show a clip of a great athlete or performer who focuses on eating well, exercising, and getting enough rest, even when tempted to spend time in less profitable ways. I may show a clip of a person being hit by another person and not returning the blow. The 1982 movie, *Gandhi*, has several examples of self-control.
- Ask the children to select a movie that has a main character with a lot of self-control, so we can watch the movie together and discuss it.

HOW I PLAN TO FIND OUT IF THEY KNOW AND DO WHAT I WANT THEM TO
- Hold one-on-one interviews using the *Progress Tracker* to determine what they know about the importance of developing self-control and how well they are improving self-discipline. Ask, "What areas in your life do you control?" (Money? Exercise? Eating? Studying?)

HOW I PLAN TO REINFORCE WHAT I HAVE TAUGHT
- At dinner every evening, we will ask the children to give examples of problems that can result from not having self-control or benefits that can result from having it.
- Visibly post a sign that says, "It's not always easy or fun to be in control, but it's worth it."
- Serve a meal alongside of a favorite dessert. Ask why the meal should be eaten first.
- Make a chart for each child to track how well he or she is improving self-discipline. The chart could have a column indicating what the child plans to do every day to improve his or her self-control and a place to indicate that he or she accomplished the tasks.

PRACTICING SELF-DIRECTED CHANGE

WHAT I WANT THEM TO KNOW
- Our family values encompass self-directed change.
- Engaging in self-directed change is important.
- We can engage in self-directed change by using the *Personal Enhancement Planner* (PEP).

WHAT I WANT THEM TO DO
- Make a change using the *Personal Enhancement Planner* (PEP)

WHAT I PLAN TO TEACH
- Our family values self-improvement.

"No man can run away from weakness. He must eventually either defeat it or perish. And if that is so … why not now, and where you stand?" (Robert Louis Stevenson)

"A simple reality, which is ignored at a terrible price, is that most human misery can be prevented by wise and disciplined living." (Victor Brown)

- You should continually try to improve yourself by identifying and overcoming weaknesses and by setting goals to accomplish things in your life that will make you a better and more capable person. This will enable you to live to your full potential.
- There is a process that can help you improve called the *Personal Enhancement Planner.*
- Using this process can make self-directed change easier and fun.

HOW I PLAN TO TEACH IT (MY METHODS)

- Ask the children why change is important, what changes they have made, and what changes they would like to make.
- Tell story about an individual who has made considerable changes in spite of opposition.
- Read quotes and lecture on points made above.
- Review the PEP with an example.
- Ask everyone to select something he or she wants to change about himself or herself and to complete a PEP before the next lesson.
- Ask them to go over their change plan at the next family meeting.

HOW I PLAN TO FIND OUT IF THEY KNOW AND DO WHAT I WANT THEM TO

- Hold one-on-one interviews using the *Progress Tracker* to determine what they know about the importance of change and how to do it systematically.
- Observe children's behavior to determine whether or not they have incorporated the PEP principles into their lives.

HOW I PLAN TO REINFORCE WHAT I HAVE TAUGHT

- Post the above quotes where everyone can see them. Talk about the quotes and what it means to change.
- Set an example of self-directed change and talk about my own progress with the PEP.

ATTACHMENT
THE PERSONAL ENHANCEMENT PLANNER

A) DETERMINE WHAT YOU WANT TO CHANGE.

Self-Improvement requires changing your behavior by either 1) adding a positive behavior like exercise, or 2) eliminating a negative behavior like oversleeping. To begin self-improvement, select the behavior you want to change. Evaluate the behavior to ensure the change you plan to make is consistent with your personal standards of right and wrong. If the change requires you to go against your personal standards, then select another behavior to work on. If the behavior does fit, and if it "feels like it's the right thing," go on to the next step.

B) MAKE A COMMITMENT TO YOURSELF BY WRITING A CHANGE GOAL.

I will (describe the behavior you plan to add or eliminate)

_____

_____

on or before (date by which you will have maintained this change for at least 21 days)_____.

I will begin preparing for this change on _____. I will have completed my preparation

by _____. I will begin changing on (date)_____.

C) PREPARE TO CHANGE.

List the things you need to begin and maintain the change. These items include obtaining information (from a credible source), skills, resources (equipment, food, books), permission, etc. Also, list where or from whom you will get these things, and when you will get them. If possible, interview someone, read a book about someone, or watch a movie about someone who made a similar change.

• WHAT DO I NEED?

• WHERE OR FROM WHOM WILL I GET WHAT I NEED?

• WHEN WILL I GET THESE THINGS?

D) DEVELOP YOUR FIRST PLAN FOR CHANGE.

List the steps (small, realistic, achievable) for improvement. Also indicate when you will take these steps (e.g., several times a day, daily, or weekly).

• WHAT I WILL DO?

• WHEN I WILL DO IT?

E) GET SUPPORT FOR CHANGE.

Although the change process is ultimately your responsibility, it can be very helpful to get support from others. Ask one or more people to help you improve. Those who agree to participate should read and sign your improvement strategy.

1. I (name of supporter)_____, agree to provide support and encouragement to (your name)_____, in his or her efforts to make the change described above. My support will include:_____.

2. I (name of supporter) _____, agree to provide support and encouragement to (your name) _____, in his or her efforts to make the change described above. My support will include:_____.

F) PLAN TO REWARD YOURSELF WHEN YOU MAKE CHANGES.
Rewarding your changes can help you maintain the change. Develop a list of rewards (that are inexpensive and unrelated to food or drugs/alcohol) that you can treat yourself to upon completing each step in your improvement process. Indicate when you will get rewards and under what conditions.

G) VISUALIZE AND LIST THE BENEFITS OF MAKING THIS CHANGE.
Visualizing the benefits (positive outcomes) you expect to gain from making this change will motivate you and help you to remain focused on what you want to accomplish. List these benefits here.

H) VISUALIZE AND LIST THE NEGATIVE CONSEQUENCES OF NOT MAKING THIS CHANGE.
Visualizing the negative outcomes you could face if you do not make this change will motivate you and help you to remain focused on what you do want to accomplish. List these possible negative outcomes here.

I) ANTICIPATE AND LIST THE OBSTACLES TO MAKING THIS CHANGE, AND WHAT YOU CAN DO TO OVERCOME THEM.
Anticipating and developing strategies to overcome obstacles can help you avoid setbacks. List thoughts, behaviors, or excuses that may be barriers to making this change. Also, list external barriers (people, places, things) that may stand in the way of your improvement.

NOTE: If you listed negative thoughts as obstacles to change, refer to the Sample Lesson on thought management strategy using the Attachment, the **Cognition Assessment and Change Strategy,** included in SAMPLE LESSON PLAN #21.

J) DETERMINE AND LIST THOSE THINGS IN YOUR LIFE YOU THAT YOU NEED TO ALTER ABOUT YOURSELF OR YOUR ENVIRONMENT TO MAKE THE CHANGE.

K) WRITE A DAILY ROUTINE FOR CHANGE.
Every day, begin your self-improvement process by doing the following:
1. Visualize the benefits you will get from changing, and the negative consequences if you do not change.
2. Review barriers you may encounter and strategies you will use to overcome them.
3. Review the steps listed in your PEP change strategy and then list those steps you will take action on today (you can list these items on a 3x5 Daily Action Card you can carry with you throughout the day).
4. Follow through consistently and repetitively on the steps you listed on your Daily Action Card.
5. After the change process begins, become aware of unforeseen things that impede your progress; record these as they come up, along with strategies for countering them.
6. When faced with barriers, counter them.
7. Track your progress by keeping a daily log where you record your daily successes, failures and strategies for overcoming them, insights and lessons learned, and so on (EMPHASIZE YOUR SUCCESSES); if your improvement plan is not working, make appropriate modifications until you "get it right"; successful change may require a number of modifications in your approach.

LEARNING TO CONTROL THOUGHTS AND PRACTICE COGNITIVE RESTRUCTURING

WHAT I WANT THEM TO KNOW
- Our thoughts are the basis of all our actions.
- Our thoughts are influenced by outside stimulus.
- We can and should control our thoughts.

WHAT I WANT THEM TO DO
- The *Cognition Assessment and Change Strategy* at the end of this lesson to help you systematically change the way they think about something.

WHAT I PLAN TO TEACH
- Our thoughts are the basis for all of our actions and are influenced by the way we interpret events and situations in our environments. The INPUT-PROCESS-OUTPUT concept explains that what we put in is what we get out:
    - If we put violent images into our minds by watching violent television, we will have violent thoughts and be more aggressive than we otherwise would have been.
    - If we expose ourselves to explicit sexual stimuli through movies, pornography, or television, we will be more inclined to have sexual thoughts and feelings and, in turn, be more inclined to act on these.

- If we hope to make changes in our lives, we need to learn to control our thoughts, because they are the basis of all our actions.

"As a person thinks in their heart, so are they." (Proverbs 23:7)

- You should be discriminating about the kinds of media you willingly expose yourself to.
- You can and should control your thoughts.
- An effective way to change your thoughts is to use the *Cognition Assessment and Change Strategy*.
- As a family, we should each select a pattern of thinking that we want to change and, in turn, work on changing it via this strategy.

HOW I PLAN TO TEACH IT (MY METHODS)
- Ask, "What role do our thoughts have in our lives?"
- Ask, "How do our thoughts influence our behavior?"
- Ask, "What things influence our thoughts?"
- Ask if anyone has thoughts that prevent him or her from doing the things he or she wants to do.
- Ask if anyone has made changes that required him or her to change his or her thoughts?
- Show a picture that illustrates INPUT-PROCESS-OUTPUT concept or GARBAGE IN, GARBAGE OUT (which is abbreviated as GIGO).
- Lecture on all the points made above.
- Describe and give an example of how to use the *Cognition Assessment and Change Strategy* to change the way they think about something.
- Challenge the children to use this strategy and report back to the family at our next meeting.

HOW I PLAN TO FIND OUT IF THEY KNOW AND DO WHAT I WANT THEM TO
- Hold one-on-one interviews using the *Progress Tracker* to determine what each child knows and does about thought control.
- Ask them if they have used the strategy and, if so, what their experiences have been like.
- Observe the kinds of media they expose themselves to and encourage positive options.

HOW I PLAN TO REINFORCE WHAT I HAVE TAUGHT

• Post a GIGO sign with some examples such as, "If you watch garbage on TV, you're going to think about garbage. Don't be a garbage collector." (Be creative here.)
• Talk about the thought pattern I am trying to change via the change strategy.
• Ask them to report back on their success at making changes.

COGNITION ASSESSMENT AND CHANGE STRATEGY

1. Become aware of the connection between environmental stimuli, thoughts, and behavior.
2. Determine which thoughts encourage the negative feelings and behavior you are going to change, or discourage the positive feelings and behavior you wish to adopt.
3. Label these "negative thoughts."
4. Decide, in advance, on thoughts you will use to replace negative thoughts that arise, and label these as "proxy thoughts."
5. Monitor negative thoughts and feelings.
6. Replace automatic negative thoughts with pre-determined replacement thoughts.
7. Determine stimuli, such as certain environments, people, or situations that trigger negative thoughts.
8. Label these "negative stimuli."
9. Decide, in advance, how you will modify, change, remove, or avoid negative stimuli.
10. Monitor negative stimuli and deal with them in accordance with what you decided to do in the previous step.
11. Continue until you no longer experience the negative thoughts you are trying to extinguish.

"My mother taught me very early to believe I could achieve any accomplishment I wanted to. The first was to walk without braces." (Wilma Rudolph, three-time Olympic gold medal winner)

ACQUIRING THE DIMENSIONS OF HEALTH AND WELL-BEING

WHAT I WANT THEM TO KNOW

- We are multi-dimensional people. We have physical, mental, social, emotional, and spiritual dimensions.
- As healthy people, we strive to live balanced lives by paying attention to our different dimensions.
- There are certain things we need to be happy, healthy, whole people.
- When we are happy and whole people, we can be more loving and supportive family members.

WHAT I WANT THEM TO DO

- Write a self-improvement plan that addresses all of the dimensions we discuss
- Apply the plan for two weeks

WHAT I PLAN TO TEACH

- All people are multi-dimensional beings: social, physical, intellectual, emotional, spiritual. (See the description of the five dimensions of well-being at the end of this lesson.)
- We all have needs in these areas.
- These needs must be satisfied to ensure that we have good health and well-being.
- If you are not whole, then you cannot reach your full potential in contributing to the overall well-being of the family.
- There is a positive relationship between your overall well-being and the extent to which your needs are satisfied in your social, physical, emotional, intellectual, and spiritual dimensions.

- The relationship between needs and personal well-being is cumulative. That is, if your needs are met on a consistent basis in these areas, you will be healthier and happier (over time) than you would be otherwise. For example, if you hope to be physically fit, you must engage in aerobic exercise on a regular basis. If you do not exercise aerobically on a regular basis, your conditioning will not improve but diminish over time.
- The relationship between your well-being and having your needs met in these areas is also synergistic, which means the combined effect of consistently meeting your needs (in the various dimensions of your being) is greater than the effect of only working on one or two areas at a time. This is due to the interrelationships among these dimensions. For example, a sedentary person who begins exercising on a regular basis experiences an improvement in both mental and physical health.
- We challenge you to write a self-improvement plan and implement the plan for two weeks. The plan should state an action that you will take each day to meet your needs in each of the five areas. For example, you might decide to: 1) (physical) walk one mile every evening, 2) (intellectual) read one chapter of a good book, 3) (emotional) spend 10 minutes relaxing, 4) (social) say hi to five people you do not know, and 5) (spiritual) pray in the morning and at night.
- If every person in our family consistently strives to improve in these five areas, we will establish and maintain a balance in our lives that will make us more loving and supportive family members. It will also help each of us live to our full potential.

  You will be smarter, stronger, better looking, you will feel better, and, as the U.S. Army commercials put it, you will "be all you that you can be." Most importantly, the overall quality of you life will improve.

  To illustrate our point more fully, I offer an analogy from a television commercial aired several years ago, sponsored by the people who produce Frahm Oil Filters. In this commercial, a mechanic holds up an oil filter that costs less than $10 and, pointing to the filter, explains the importance of using a good filter and changing your filter on a regular basis. The mechanic ends his spiel by saying, "Pay *me now or pay me later," at which point he turns and points to an automobile up on a lift that is obviously getting a major overhaul. The commercial's message is that a consumer can pay a minimal amount on a regular basis by getting an oil change every X-thousand miles and avoid paying a much greater price later on. We believe this principle of "pay me now or pay me later," when applied to the concept of health and well-being, serves to illustrate the importance of consistently taking preventive actions. Accordingly, we will now apply this principle to each of the dimensions of well-being.*

HOW I PLAN TO TEACH IT (MY METHODS)
- Ask, "Do you think a person who is physically healthy is always happy?"
- Provide examples of people who are physically healthy, but who have other health problems (i.e., intellectual, mental, social, or spiritual problems).
- Make all of the above points.
- Have each person write a plan to do something every day for two weeks in each of the five areas.
- Assign them all to report back in two weeks on their self-improvement activities.
- Have everyone make and display posters that encourage family members to stick with their self-improvement goals.
- Make a video featuring family members testifying to the benefits of meeting their needs across the five dimensions.
- Make a "Let's Get High-5" poster.

HOW I PLAN TO FIND OUT IF THEY KNOW AND DO WHAT I WANT THEM TO
- Hold one-on-one interviews using the *Progress Tracker* to determine what they are doing to meet their needs in the five dimensions.
- Observe behavior and encourage children to use the family posters for encouragement.
- Listen to their reports and view their posters.

HOW I PLAN TO REINFORCE WHAT I HAVE TAUGHT
- Write and implement my own self-improvement plan.
- Share my experiences with my self-improvement plan at each family meeting for the next two weeks.
- Take part in the family video.

- Post the "Let's Get High-5" poster.
- Share stories about individuals who have made major changes for the better.
- Read the following information about the various dimensions of well-being.

FIVE DIMENSIONS OF WELL-BEING

Physical Dimension: The effects of consistently ignoring this dimension are oftentimes more obvious than with the other dimensions. For example, at the time this book was published the National Cancer Institute, Centers for Disease Control, and the American Cancer Society all agree that a very small percentage (about 5%) of cancers are hereditary. They also agree that a vast majority of cancers are caused by things we have control over, including how we eat and whether or not we smoke. Furthermore, if we do not regularly apply self-restraint in terms of how much we eat, we can put on excess pounds and most adults know, by sad experience, the heavy price they must pay to overcome unwanted body weight.

As mentioned, it is important to our **physical** dimension that we exercise on a regular basis. Again, at the time this book was published exercise physiologists commonly agree that exercising aerobically (walking, jogging, skating, biking, etc.) most days each week, for at least 30 minutes per session, will produce a positive beneficial effect on our heart, lungs, and blood vessels. The subsequent benefit of such a training effect can also serve to illustrate the interrelationship between the dimensions of our well-being. That is, in addition to receiving physical benefits such as reduced heart disease, lower percent body fat, lower blood pressure, lower blood cholesterol, those who engage in aerobic exercise on a regular basis also gain mental health benefits, such as improved self-esteem, enhanced perception of body image, decreased depression and anxiety, as well as social benefits, such as a fuller social life because of an enhanced appearance and zest for living. In fact, researchers in California (Belloc and Breslow, 1972) who were among the first to examine the benefits of a healthy lifestyle studied the lives of 7,000 men and women found a relationship between physical well-being and years of life lived and adherence to seven basic practices: sleeping seven to eight hours every night, eating three meals a day at regular times with little snacking, eating breakfast every day, maintaining desirable body weight, avoiding excessive alcohol consumption, getting regular exercise, and not smoking. This report also indicated that men at age 45 who follow three or fewer of these practices can expect to live to 67; men in the same age group who follow six to seven of these practices could expect to live to 78. Similarly, women at age 45 who follow three or fewer of these practices can expect to live to 74, while women who abide by six or seven of these practices can expect to live to 81.

Emotional Dimension: The "pay me now or pay me later" concept can also be applied to **mental** health. This is illustrated in the following figure referred to here as Cole's Coping Continuum. As with the Parenting Logic Model introduced at the beginning of this book, this diagram illustrates how our responses to the stress caused by the day-to-day problems we encounter in life can make us emotionally stronger or weaker.

In the context of this Continuum (viewing from left to right), problems are those things we encounter on a daily basis that cause us stress. They come in all sizes, from small to overwhelmingly large. From a psychological perspective, problems are those things we register in our minds as discrepancies between the way things are and the way we would like them to be. In a broad sense, a problem exists when an individual becomes aware of a significant difference between what they want to experience in life and what actually happens to them. For example, if you wake up with pain in your shoulder and you don't want to experience pain (only the true masochist does) then you have a problem–you are experiencing pain. If the undesirable pain is great, the discrepancy between your desire to be like "most people," pain free, is great. Therefore, you have a big problem which will cause stress and motivate you to cope.

It follows that when a person experiences a problem, they also experience stress. Stress (again, viewing the Figure from left to

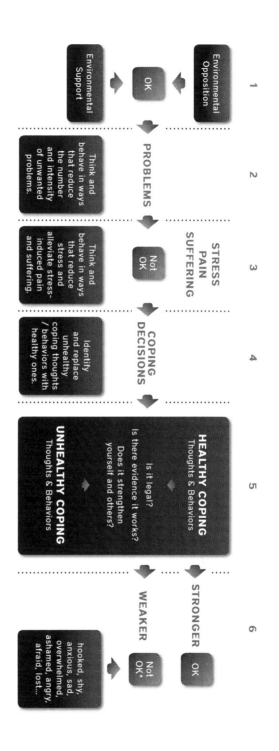

1

Environmental
Opposition

Ok

Environmental
Support

2 PROBLEMS

Think and
behave in ways
that reduce
the number
and intensity
of unwanted
problems.

3 STRESS PAIN SUFFERING

Not
OK

Think and
behave in ways
that reduce
stress and
alleviate stress-
induced pain
and suffering.

4 COPING DECISIONS

Identify
and replace
unhealthy
coping thoughts
/ behaviors with
healthy ones.

5

HEALTHY COPING
Thoughts & Behaviors

Is it legal?
Does it strengthen
yourself and others?
Is there evidence it works?

UNHEALTHY COPING
Thoughts & Behaviors

6 STRONGER

OK

WEAKER

Not
OK*

hooked, shy,
anxious, sad,
overwhelmed,
ashamed, angry,
afraid, lost...

*Crisis Response: Call a friend, 911, a hotline, or your higher power; Meet with a therapist;
Go to the nearest hospital emergency room; Take a cold shower; Attend a 12-step group

right) is a form of either psychological or physical pain. In the most basic sense, it's a message to our brain that something is wrong. As with problems, humans experience stress from birth. This is true in every race and culture on planet earth. Finally, because stress is a form of pain and because we are programmed from birth to react to pain, when humans experience stress caused by a problem (things are not the way they want them to be) they begin coping in an effort to reduce the pain. As an infant the coping response is crying. As we get older, our coping responses become more varied and deliberate. And, in every case, the coping responses we engage in are designed to remove the pain. For example, if we have normal sensation in our fingers and we touch a hot stove we quickly pull back in response to the pain. Similarly, if we feel uncomfortable in a social situation we want to exit.

The point in all of this is that the way we cope over time will determine whether or not we are getting emotionally stronger or weaker. Those who prefer "quick fixes" to stress, like drinking to relax, or smoking marijuana to forget, or quitting a job to escape an uncomfortable workplace, or retreating from a stressful situation like giving a public presentation, tend to become emotionally weaker over time. Whereas, those who apply healthy coping mechanisms like exercise, meditation, seeking help from others, etc., will tend to become more emotionally resilient over time.

Intellectual Dimension: Development or lack of development of our intellect also plays a role in well-being. If your child does not "pay now" by consistently studying, getting good grades in school, and gaining new and diverse information—particularly in our highly specialized and technological society—he or she will likely pay the price later of under- or unemployment and will likely need major retraining (the overhaul). Because we live in an age when the proliferation of information is occurring at an unprecedented rate, one of the most important skills you can teach your children is how to engage in self-directed learning. Consequently, we have included lessons on some of the best ways to acquire knowledge on specific topics of interest.

Social Dimension: Without a doubt, our **social** development or adeptness is key to our health and well-being. If you do not pay the price to teach your child good social skills, he or she may not learn to interact appropriately with peers, teachers, and eventually employers. The costs associated with not acquiring these skills can include an inability to resist peer pressure, lack of general assertiveness, inability to make and keep friends, marital problems, and being passed over for desirable jobs or promotions.

Spiritual Dimension: Considerable research in recent years has documented what prophets and wise men have passed down through the ages: attention or lack of attention to our **spiritual** and **character development** dimension can and does have a measurable impact on our health and well-being. If your child does not learn to meet his or her needs in this area through such activities as meditation and prayer (see Sample Lesson #25), reading inspirational literature, learning the difference between good and bad/right and wrong, and serving others in the community, he or she can become spiritually malnourished and will be unprepared when confronted with the life crises that we all encounter.

Multi-Dimensional Considerations: If addressed appropriately and on a consistent basis, these dimensions can increase the likelihood that your family (as a whole and as individual members) will be functional and happy. It should be noted, however, that to attain and maintain balance, the pursuit of meeting these needs should always be looked at as a means to an end rather than an end in itself. People who become preoccupied with popularity, status, or physical appearance lose perspective and become imbalanced in their approach to living. Although it is not a bad thing to focus attention on one area or another, balance across all of these dimensions should be considered the ideal means toward the end of becoming a healthy person with character.

THINKING AND FEELING: THE KEY TO POSITIVE EMOTIONS

WHAT I WANT THEM TO KNOW

- The way the members of a family think impacts how its individuals feel and how the family functions.
- You can change the way you feel by changing the way you think.
- You can use the *Thought Restructuring Form* to help you replace your self-discouraging thoughts with self-encouraging thoughts.

WHAT I WANT THEM TO DO

- Think in ways that contribute to positive emotions
- Think in ways that help them relate positively toward other family members

WHAT I PLAN TO TEACH

- The way the members of a family think impacts how its individuals feel and how the family functions. If you have thought patterns that run counter to feeling good about yourself and other family members, both you and our family will be negatively impacted.
- Monitor your emotions throughout the day. When you start feeling negative emotions, record them in column 1 of the *Thought Restructuring Form*, and examine what you think in connection with these emotions.
- If you are thinking negative thoughts, replace your self-discouraging thoughts with self-encouraging thoughts. On the *Thought Restructuring Form*, record discouraging thoughts in column 2 and encouraging thoughts in column 3.

- The information you have recorded on this form is your plan for overcoming your negative emotions. Implement the plan by consistently replacing self-discouraging thoughts with the replacement thoughts recorded in column 3.

THOUGHT RESTRUCTURING GUIDE: PART 1

The way you think and the things you do have an impact on your emotions and sense of well-being. If you hold on to irrational beliefs (see Reference 2) and/or you think negative thoughts, you will feel negative emotions (see Reference 1). Consequently, to decrease your negative emotions you can replace irrational beliefs and thoughts that cause unpleasant feelings with thoughts that produce more positive emotions.

The *Thought Restructuring Guide* is designed to help you identify and replace thoughts and thought patterns that cause unpleasant emotions. Part 1 of this guide will help you monitor and evaluate your thoughts as they relate to your negative emotions. Tables A and B below are designed to help your organize yourself as you go through this thought restructuring process.

To start the process complete the following steps: 1) monitor your emotions throughout the day, 2) record negative emotions in Column 1, Table A, 3) in column 2, record the time and context of what is going on at the time you notice the negative emotions, 4) determine which thoughts are associated with the emotions listed in Column 1, 5) record negative thoughts in Column 3, 6) evaluate each thought recorded in Column 3 by answering the questions in Column 4. After completing Table A, go on to Table B where you will record replacement thoughts for the irrational and distorted thoughts you have recorded in Column 3, Table A.

TABLE A: THOUGHT RECORD				
Negative Emotions (Examples of Negative Emotions are Listed below in Reference 1)	Day/Time/ Event (When did you notice the negative emotion and what was going on around the same time?)	Related Thoughts (The Thoughts You are Thinking When you Are Upset)	Evaluate Your Thoughts (These Are Rules That Will Help you Referee Your Thoughts)	
			Is it Rational? (See Reference 2)	Is it Distorted? (See Reference 3)

REFERENCE 1
COMMON NEGATIVE EMOTIONS
Embarrassed, guilty, angry, sad, incompetent, afraid, anxious, hopeless, unhappy, disappointed, pessimistic, frustrated, regretful, lonely, inferior, panicky, worthless

REFERENCE 2
IRRATIONAL THINKING
Irrational thinking includes thoughts that are 1) not based on fact, 2) do not help you feel the way you want to feel, and 3) do not help you achieve your goals. According to behavioral scientists, the most common irrational thoughts among Americans are as follows (Albert Ellis, http://www.rebt.org):

1. It is a dire necessity for me to be loved or approved by almost all others, who are significant to me.
2. I must be thoroughly competent, adequate, and achieving, in all important respects, in order to be worthwhile.
3. The world must be fair. People must act fairly and considerately and if they don't, they are bad, wicked, villainous, or incredibly stupid; they should be severely blamed and punished.
4. It is awful and terrible when things are not the way I very much want them to be.

5. There isn't much I can do about my anxiety, anger depression, or unhappiness, because my feelings are caused by what happens to me.
6. If something is dangerous or dreadful, I should be constantly and excessively upset about it and should dwell on the possibility of its occurring.
7. It is easier to avoid and to put off facing life's difficulties and responsibilities than face them.
8. I'm quite dependent on others and need someone stronger than myself to rely upon; I can't run my own life.
9. My past history mainly causes my present feelings and behavior; things from my past, which once strongly influenced me, will always strongly influence me.
10. I must become very anxious, angry, or depressed over someone else's problems and disturbances, if I care about that person.
11. There is a right and perfect solution to almost all problems, and it is awful not to find it.

REFERENCE 3
COGNITIVE DISTORTIONS – THOUGHT VIRUSES

Irrational thoughts are sometimes labeled as cognitive distortions. Cognitive distortions are patterns of thinking that produce illogical thoughts that oftentimes produce negative emotions. The 10 most common cognitive distortions are (What Are Cognitive Distortions? By Nancy Schimelpfening, _www.About.com_ Guide, Updated September 27, 2007):

1. **ALL OR NOTHING THINKING**
    Thinking in black and white when many legitimate alternatives exist.
2. **OVER-GENERALISATION**
    Pretending that everything can be judged by a single occurrence or person etc. Trying to "tar everything with the same brush."
3. **MENTAL FILTER**
    Seeing only the bad so you lose your perspective. Not widening your focus.
4. **DISQUALIFYING THE POSITIVE**
    As it says, this is the way the mind justifies inner-philosophies that make you unhappy.

5. **JUMPING TO CONCLUSIONS (A) - MIND READING ERROR**
Assuming people think a certain thing when you have no evidence for that.

6. **JUMPING TO CONCLUSIONS (B) FORTUNE-TELLING ERROR**
Assuming that a certain thing will happen when you've got no evidence for that.

7. **MAGNIFICATION/MINIMALISATION**
Blowing things out of proportion, or minimalizing the good aspects in yourself or a situation.

8. **EMOTIONAL REASONING**
Taking things personally when they weren't meant that way.

9. **SHOULD STATEMENTS**
Feeling things should be a certain way that you think best - and letting it get to you when they are not.

10. **LABELLING/MISLABELLING**
Labeling yourself or someone else, rather than seeing them for the whole person they are.

11. **PERSONALIZATION**
Thinking that things turn bad because you yourself are bad.

THOUGHT RESTRUCTURING GUIDE: PART 2
The second part of this guide is designed to systematically help you replace irrational and distorted thoughts and thought patterns. Place all of the distorted and irrational thoughts you recorded in Table A, in Column 1 of Table B. Decide on new thoughts you can use to counter the irrational thoughts listed in Column 1, 2) list your replacement thoughts in Column 2, and 3) in Columns 3 and 4, respectively, develop a practice schedule for overcoming your irrational thinking. Share your progress with your therapist.

TABLE B: "REPLACEMENT THOUGHT" PRACTICE SCHEDULE			
Irrational and/ or Distorted Thoughts (Taken from Column 3, in Table A)	Rational Replacement Thoughts	When and Where I Will Practice New Rational Thinking	How Often I Will Practice

HOW I PLAN TO TEACH IT (MY METHODS)

- I will use a lecture to help children distinguish between positive and negative thoughts.
- I will demonstrate how to use the *Thought Restructuring Form*.
- I will assign each family member who is old enough to use the form for one week.

HOW I PLAN TO FIND OUT IF THEY KNOW AND DO WHAT I WANT THEM TO

- Hold one-on-one interviews using the *Progress Tracker* to determine if they are replacing negative emotions and thoughts with positive ones.
- Ask each family member to report at the next family meeting how he or she did with the *Thought Restructuring Form*.

HOW I PLAN TO REINFORCE WHAT I HAVE TAUGHT

- I will set an example by using the *Thought Restructuring Form* and reporting to my family on my own successes and failures.
- Every week in our family meeting, a family member will be assigned to read or recite an encouraging thought that can be used to replace self-discouraging thinking.

DEVELOPING PROBLEM SOLVING

WHAT I WANT THEM TO KNOW

- We all experience problems.
- We can learn to solve problems effectively and teach others to do the same.
- Complaining about problems is not an effective way to solve them and can even be counterproductive.
- Life is not fair. Many of the problems we experience are caused by others.
- If we become good at solving problems, we will be highly valued by society and will experience a greater sense of well-being.
- *The Serenity Prayer* offers guidance to help us solve and accept problems.

WHAT I WANT THEM TO DO

- Accept that everyone has problems
- Adopt and apply a systematic approach to solving problems

WHAT I PLAN TO TEACH

- All families and individuals have problems. It is irrational to think otherwise.
- Problems are a discrepancy between what we want and what we experience.
- Complaining about problems is not an effective way to solve them and can be counterproductive.
- Life is not fair. Many of the problems we experience are caused by others. If we accept these problems as a challenge and work through them, we can become good at solving problems.

- People who are good at solving problems are highly valued by society and experience a greater sense of well-being because 1) they accept the rational idea that all people have problems, 2) they are not afraid of the challenge that problems present, 3) they have learned to effectively solve their problems and thereby reduce the stress that accompanies them, and 4) they have learned to be patient and/or accepting when problems are not readily resolved.
- The Serenity Prayer: *God grant me the serenity to accept the things I cannot change, the courage to change the things I can, and the wisdom to know the difference.*
- You can learn to solve problems effectively and teach others to do the same. There are many good problem-solving approaches that you can use to identify and overcome familial and individual problems. One good approach is to use the *Problem Solving Planner*, or PSP (see Table 22.1). This tool has two phases.
- Phase I of the PSP directs you to 1) identify the problem, 2) define it, 3) investigate to determine the causes and possible solutions, 4) decide which causes you will address and which action steps you will take to alleviate these causes, and 5) establish a schedule for monitoring progress and getting feedback that can be used to improve the strategy. In Phase II you put the information together to make up your intervention strategy. An example of how the PSP can be applied in overcoming the problem of low grades in school is described as follows.

PHASE I - UNDERSTANDING THE PROBLEM

Step 1 : Assume you want to help your child raise low grades. You expect your child to get As and Bs in school but he or she is getting Cs, Ds, and Fs. Your child has a problem; *you* have a problem.

Step 2: You define the problem as, "We expect you to get all As and Bs on your report card and you got a D in your Political Systems class. You have a problem. We will help you identify what is causing your problem and what steps you can take to overcome it." (Note that although you have agreed to help identify a strategy for overcoming the problem, you have placed ownership of the problem on your son/daughter.)

<u>Step 3:</u> You talk to your child and your child's Political Systems teacher to determine what is causing the problem. Your child says the reasons why she is not doing well in the class are that she does not like the class, the teacher is boring, and she does not see how the class can help her in the future. On the other hand, the teacher says your child is having difficulties with the class because she does not pay attention to the class lectures, and therefore she does not take good notes which, in turn, means she cannot prepare for the tests. You talk to your child further and discover she has difficulty taking notes because the teacher lectures very fast and she cannot keep up. You ask your daughter if she has any good friends in the class who might be willing to share their notes. You find out that she does not know anyone in the class on a personal level (another potential problem). Because there are still nine weeks left in the class, you talk to the school to find out whether or not your child can be transferred to another Political Systems class. You are told no. You then visit the local library and check out a book on note-taking.

<u>Step 4:</u> You surmise that the two causes of the problem that you will help your daughter address are 1) lack of perceived relevancy of the class, and 2) difficulty with note-taking. Although it may be true that your daughter's teacher is indeed boring, because this is beyond your control, you decide not to work on this potential cause. However, you do decide to make the point to your daughter that if she will apply herself and learn more about the subject, then she may be more interested in what the teacher has to say. (Make this suggestion after dealing with the other problems, so your daughter will not think that you are siding with the teacher. Your daughter needs to know you are firmly in her corner and that you will help her resolve her problem.) Whether or not the teacher is boring is irrelevant because neither of you can do anything about that. Only work on those things that you have power over, and choose teachers more wisely in the future.

TABLE 22.1: THE PROBLEM-SOLVING PLANNER

PHASE I: UNDERSTANDING THE PROBLEM

Step 1: Identify the Problem
A problem is a "gap" between what should be happening and what is actually happening in the life of your children. For example, if you want your child to get As and Bs in school but he or she is getting Cs, Ds, and Fs, your child has a problem.

Step 2: Define the Problem
Clearly stating the problem you plan to work on is essential to focus on what it is that you plan to change.

Step 3: Investigate to Determine the Causes and Possible Solutions
If you can determine what is causing the problem, then you will be able to focus your attention on the causes rather than the symptoms.

Step 4: Decide Which Causes to Address and Which Steps to Take to Alleviate Them
Once you know what the problem is, and what is causing it, you will be able to select the appropriate action steps to address each cause.

Step 5: Establish a Schedule for Monitoring Progress and Getting Feedback
You must follow up to ensure that each action step is executed.

PHASE II: YOUR INTERVENTION STRATEGY

Cause to Be Addressed (Step 3)	Action Steps (Step 4)	When Actions Are Completed (Step 5)

As a plan of action, you decide to watch two politically-oriented videos with your daughter and have a guided discussion after each video. You also plan to do research to explain all the ways in which political systems can influence her life. In addition, you make the point that knowing about these systems gives her the power to influence or change them, if they ever do have a negative impact on her life. You also decide to read, with your child, the library book on note-taking. Finally, you indicate to your daughter that you will go over her Political Systems notes with her every day after school to determine whether or not she is improving in her note-taking abilities. You also promise to reward her progress with something that she really wants (the motivating incentive).

Step 5: A plan for following up might be to always meet with your daughter immediately after she gets home from school to examine her notes and read with her from the book about note-taking. At this time, you can monitor her progress and determine whether anything else can be done to help her overcome this problem. You can also remind her (when you see that she is making progress) that she is earning a special surprise. Let her know when she will receive this reward. For example, you could say, "I will give you your reward three weeks from today if you continue to make progress." (Be specific.)

PHASE II – YOUR INTERVENTION STRATEGY

As indicated above, in Phase II of the PSP you put your strategy together. The matrix that follows will help you do this in a systematic way. In column 1, you list what you perceive to be the causes of the problem. In column 2, you describe the action steps you will take in connection with each cause. Finally, in column 3 you record information about when the action steps will be completed. The example described in Phase I is organized in this matrix.

Cause to Be Addressed (Step 3)	Action Steps (Step 4)	When Actions Are Completed (Step 5)
Lack of Perceived Relevancy	Show interesting videos like Mr. Smith goes to Washington and Gandhi. After the videos, I will lead a guided discussion on how politics can have an influence on my daughter's life. On Monday, I will call and reserve the videos I have chosen to watch. I will prepare a number of questions to help guide our discussion.	I will view the selected videos with my daughter this Saturday and next Tuesday night. I will ask her the guiding questions immediately after watching the videos and throughout the next week to reinforce my points.
Poor Note-taking Skills	My daughter and I will read and take notes on the book, The ABCs of Note-taking. I will review my daughter's Political Systems notes every day after school and give her credit toward something special if she shows progress.	We will read every evening before she does her homework. If considerable progress is made (be specific about what you mean by progress), I will give my daughter her reward three weeks from a set date (be specific).

Once I have taught my children the problem-solving logic described above, I will teach them a second, more abbreviated form of problem-solving. The steps in this abbreviated approach are as follows:

• List all your problems and concerns on a piece of paper.
• Write each problem on a separate 3X5 card.
• Rank each problem, from most to least important, by putting the

most important card on top and the least important card on the bottom. Number the cards sequentially.

- On every card, write steps that you can take to solve the problem.
- Review the problems at least three times every day: morning, midday, and night. As you review the problems, try to think of action steps you can take to solve them. List any additional action steps that may be helpful.
- Carry the cards with you at all times so when ideas come to you about how to solve a particular problem, you can stop and record them.
- Once a day, spend some time meditating on your most important problems.

HOW I PLAN TO TEACH IT (MY METHODS)
- I will use lecture, a group activity, and examples to help children identify a problem and how they can solve it with our help.
- We will work through two problems using the tools described above.

HOW I PLAN TO FIND OUT IF THEY KNOW AND DO WHAT I WANT THEM TO
- Hold one-on-one interviews using the *Progress Tracker* to determine what children know and do about the problem-solving guidance I have provided them.

HOW I PLAN TO REINFORCE WHAT I HAVE TAUGHT
- When children are struggling with a problem, ask them if they have gone through the problem-solving process I taught them.
- When I experience problems that can be shared with my children, I will explain how I used to problem-solving methods mentioned above to address the problems.

INCREASING SPIRITUALITY AND USING PRAYER

WHAT I WANT THEM TO KNOW
- Prayer can help you in many ways.
- There is a proper way to pray.
- There are many times during the day that you can pray.
- You can pray for many things.

WHAT I WANT THEM TO DO
- Have formal prayers every morning and every night
- Informally conduct silent prayers when they need help or when they want to express gratitude for blessings
- Participate in family prayer on a daily basis
- Encourage others to pray
- Do their part to ensure that their prayers are answered

WHAT I PLAN TO TEACH
- Prayer is direct communication with God.
- You pray as follows (please adapt this to your understanding of how to pray). We have taught our children to pray the following way:
    - Address God (e.g., Our Father in Heaven).
    - Thank Him for your blessings (e.g., a nice teacher, health, loving parents, a new bike).
    - Express sorrow and ask forgiveness for failings, and express a desire to do better.
    - Ask for the things you need (e.g., encouragement, understanding or knowledge, more engergy, help with overcoming a problem).
    - Close the prayer.
- Prayer can help in many ways. Through prayer, you can obtain greater peace, guidance, comfort, encouragement, courage, insight, protection, more control over your passions (like your temper), and so on.

- We should have formal prayers every morning and every night.
- You can informally conduct silent prayers when you need help (e.g., guidance, encouragement, ability to forgive someone) or when you want to express gratitude for blessings.
- You should participate in family prayers on a daily basis.
- You can encourage others to pray.
- Do your part to ensure that your prayers are answered. This is illustrated in a quote by Abraham Lincoln: he "prayed like everything depended on God and worked like everything depended on him."
- Each member of our family should commit to prayer.

HOW I PLAN TO TEACH IT (MY METHODS)
- Explain what prayer is.
- Explain the benefits of prayer.
- Ask family members to share positive experiences with prayer.
- Read quotes of famous people who have prayed.
- Read from a children's book on prayer.
- Read or tell a story about a famous person who prayed (for example, George Washington).
- Show a movie where a main character benefits from prayer.
- Ask children to pray faithfully for one week and have them report back on the things they learned about prayer.
- Model the proper steps of prayer during family prayer time.
- Begin and/or end family meetings with prayer.
- Pray before meals.

HOW I PLAN TO FIND OUT IF THEY KNOW AND DO WHAT I WANT THEM TO
- Hold one-on-one interviews using the *Progress Tracker* to determine what my children know and do about the instructions we have given them on prayer.

HOW I PLAN TO REINFORCE WHAT I HAVE TAUGHT
- Hold family prayer every morning and night.
- Pray before meals.
- Open family meetings with prayer.
- Encourage children to volunteer to offer prayers during church services.

CHAPTER 23
CONCLUSION AND SUMMARY

As I said at the outset of this book, to ensure the best outcomes, parenting should be approached systematically. To support this idea, I have provided you with ingredients to do the job. I have given you guidance on how to effectively manage your family and train your children and the tools required to systematically do both.

Although the ideas I have supplied require an investment of time and energy, based on both my personal and professional experience, I know they will pay enormous dividends in the lives of your children. Moreover, if you set aside the time required to establish your parenting plan and do what I suggest to implement the plan (with your own modifications to fit your personal circumstances), you will accomplish a lot within the precious time you have to spend with your children. And accomplishing more with less means you are going to become a more efficient and effective parent.

REFERENCES

CAUTELA, J.R., & KASTENBAUM, R. (1967). A reinforcer survey schedule for use in therapy, training, and research. *Psychological Reports*, 20, 1115-1130.CAUTELA, J.R. (1983). The self-control triad: description and clinical applications. *Behavior Modification*, 7, 299-315.

COLE, G., FRIEDMAN, G., & BAGWELL, M. (1986). A worksite behavioral health education program based on operant conditioning. *Occupational Health Nursing*, 24(3), 132-137.

FISHBEIN, M., BANDURA, A., TRIANDIS, H.C., KAUFER, F.H., & BECKER, M.H. (1991). Factors influencing behavior and behavior change. Final report prepared for NIMH theorists workshop, Washington, D.C.

PREMACK, D. (1965). Reinforcement theory. In D. Levin (Ed.), NebraskaSymposium on Motivation. Lincoln, Nebraska: University of Nebraska Press, 123-180.

SKINNER, B.F. (1953). Science of self-control. New York: Holt, Rinehart & Winston, Inc.

ABOUT THE AUTHORS

DR GALEN E. COLE, PH.D., M.P.H., LPC

Dr. Cole is a licensed professional counselor. As a therapist, he provides individual, marriage, and family therapy. He has extensive training and experience in counseling psychology, psychiatric epidemiology, behavioral science research, education, mass and interpersonal communication, and public health.

He has taught counseling psychology, equine assisted mental health, behavioral and evaluation research, and a number of other counseling and health-related courses at the university level. He has been on the faculty at Northern Arizona University, Arizona State University, University of Idaho, Pennsylvania State University, and is currently on the graduate faculty at both the Rollins School of Public Health at Emory University in Atlanta, Georgia, and the Masters in Counseling Psychology at Prescott College, in Prescott, Arizona.

Dr. Cole has extensive experience practicing what he teaches, including working on staff and as a consultant at numerous clinics, hospitals, and community-based organizations; serving as the executive director of a not-for-profit foundation; working as an assistant director of public health in Phoenix, Arizona; and working as a behavioral scientist and director of research and evaluation activities in various centers, institutes, and offices at the U.S. Centers for Disease Control and Prevention (CDC) in Atlanta, Georgia, where he now serves as director of communications in the U.S. Office on Smoking and Health. Dr. Cole was appointed by the Governor of Georgia to serve on the Georgia Human Resources (DHR) Board. In this capacity, he served as chair of the DHR committee that provides policy guidance to the state Division of Mental Health, Developmental Disabilities, and Addictive Diseases. He has also received distinguished alumni awards from two of the universities he attended.

Dr. Cole has been a trainer and consultant in the Central Asian Republics, Nigeria, China, Thailand, Kenya, Switzerland, Australia, Peru, Germany, Uganda, and the Middle East, where he has conducted training with the Palestinian Health Authority and the Israeli Ministry of Health. He has been widely published and has made presentations at conferences and training seminars across the world.

Dr. Cole and his wife, Priscilla, have been married for over thirty years and are the parents of five children.

SKOT WALDRON

Skot is a partner at smbolic, a brand consulting and design firm with offices in Chicago, Vancouver, and Atlanta. A graduate of the Portfolio Center in Atlanta, Skot's work for clients such as Houghton Mifflin Harcourt, Sesame Workshop, Navistar, Chiquita, Manpower and Pactiv includes national and international branding campaigns as well as video, web, print, tradeshow, social media and event design. In his eight years with smbolic, Skot's work has been honored with numerous design, investor relations, and communications awards, and featured in a wide range of publications including *AIGA Communication Graphics, The AR100 Annual Report Show, Communication Arts, Applied Arts, International ARC Awards,* and *How Magazine.*

Skot currently teaches strategic branding at Portfolio Center, and speaks at various locations and businesses about the value of brands and how they pertain to us as individuals, families, and corporations.

He and his wife, Christi, have been married for eight years and are parents to a new baby girl.

Made in the USA
Charleston, SC
26 October 2010